Customer Innovation

Enjoy!

Menon

Customer Innovation

Customer-centric strategy for enduring growth

Marion Debruyne

KoganPage

LONDON PHILADELPHIA NEW DELHI

First published in Great Britain and the United States in 2014 by Kogan Page Limited
Reprinted 2014 (three times)

2nd Floor, 45 Gee Street
London EC1V 3RS
United Kingdom

1518 Walnut Street, Suite 1100
Philadelphia PA 19102
USA

4737/23 Ansari Road
Daryaganj
New Delhi 110002
India

www.koganpage.com

© Marion Debruyne, 2014

The right of Marion Debruyne to be identified as the author of this work has been asserted by her in accordance with the Copyright, Designs and Patents Act 1988.

ISBN   978 0 7494 7164 4
E-ISBN   978 0 7494 7165 1

British Library Cataloguing-in-Publication Data

A CIP record for this book is available from the British Library.

Library of Congress Cataloging-in-Publication Data

Debruyne, Marion.
  Customer innovation : customer-centric strategy for enduring growth / Marion Debruyne.
    pages cm
    ISBN 978-0-7494-7164-4 (paperback) — ISBN 978-0-7494-7165-1 (ebk)
1. Customer relations.   2. Customer services.   3. Strategic planning.   I. Title.
  HF5415.5.D43 2014
  658.8'12—dc23

                                                                                                    2014005695

Typeset by Amnet
Print production managed by Jellyfish
Printed and bound by 4edge Limited, UK

CONTENTS

Introduction
Connect-convert-collaborate

Being customer-centric and being innovative are often presented as two opposite ends of the spectrum, just as product leadership and customer intimacy are viewed as priorities that are irreconcilable. This book shows how these are false dichotomies. It shows how a new set of organizations have discovered a new formula: they combine customer-centricity with innovative power. These organizations have created a completely outside-in approach to the market. They are not driving by what they happen to be good at. They start with the market and design their strategy around it. They build and change their company completely around the customer.

They replace practices of the past with a new set of capabilities that enable them to be ahead of the curve in discovering new market opportunities. These enable them to develop new products and services faster than ever before. And they hit the bull's eye in the market. Today we are experiencing a transition point. In the past, having a disciplined innovation pipeline based on solid R&D was enough to make you an innovation master, a company admired for its innovation capabilities. Today, this is just the Olympic minimum. And it does not deliver the same success anymore.

CASE STUDY

Take for example the latest project KLM is working on. If you book a flight with KLM any day soon, you may be presented with an interactive luggage tag. This tag will allow you to seamlessly get through check-in and baggage-check, bypassing the lines of other passengers trying to get through the terminal. And at arrival, it will allow you to trace your luggage quickly. This example of high technology will make your life easier as a traveller, shaving time off the exasperating experience that modern travel is. It will make sure that your luggage never gets lost, reduce the administrative flow, and make personal communication possible with you while you are in transit before boarding the flight.

Why does an airline like KLM bother to introduce smart gadgets to their travellers? To begin with, it is all too aware of the aggravations and struggles of today's sky warriors. Its online frequent flier communities allow it to tap into customer segments on an ongoing basis. And it realizes that the overall customer experience does not start when boarding the plane, but is already going on at the airport. Creating an easy seamless airport check-in process does not only shave off time for the passenger, it also reduces the likelihood of errors. Being an airline, KLM does not possess the necessary skills to make the interactive luggage tag reality: its core business is in operating aircraft. But start-up company Fast Track Company did have the skills to make it happen. KLM initiated a partnership, and together a workable solution was prototyped.

The story of KLM shows a new approach to innovation. Companies like KLM have unlocked the keys to longevity and growth. What characterizes them? They relentlessly listen to customers. They relentlessly innovate. They adapt their business model when that is required to build the perfect customer solution. They build connections with outside parties to complement their in-house competences and enable new customer solutions. They have abandoned much of the conventional wisdom on growth and innovation. They embrace the fact that in today's fast changing world, the only way to remain on top is to constantly feel the pulse of the market. Not doing everything themselves but joining forces with others to deliver innovations to the market.

FIGURE I.1 The core processes of customer innovation

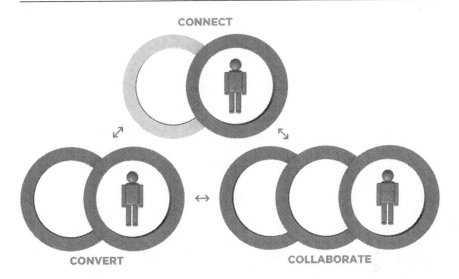

Customer innovation works backwards. Innovations are not crafted to find a 'blue ocean' market or a 'white space' opportunity. The sole and unique focus is on customer needs. Innovations are crafted to formulate a response to an unmet customer need. As a result of this exercise, organizations adapt accordingly and very often will conclude that they do not possess all the necessary skills in-house to fully deliver what the market requires. Consequently they go outside to find those that can help them accomplish the full customer solution. Collaboration is the key to deliver upon market requirements quickly and completely.

These organizations operate according to a new model. This model encompasses three building blocks that describe the processes that organizations that excel at customer innovation engage in and master exceptionally well; see Figure I.1.

Connect

First, organizations that innovate around the customer constantly connect with the market to anticipate the changes they will be confronted with. They scan the environment to pick up signals of emerging and unfulfilled customer needs. They are in constant touch with their customers, listen to them, involve them, and engage with them to understand their overall customer experience and unmet needs. They are triggered to understand the pain points of their customers but they do not become the slave of their customer base. Often there is a fear that listening intently to customers might result in inordinate attention being paid to current markets so the company fails to see emerging markets. Outside-in organizations prevent this from happening by having a wide lens for viewing the entire potential market including new or previously unaddressed segments.

Convert

Second, organizations that innovate around the customer see innovation as the only avenue for long-term survival. Every day they innovate and convert customer insights into actionable change because they believe this is the only route to stay ahead of competition, but mostly because, in order to serve customers better, you have to constantly question whether today's offerings will meet tomorrow's demands. Customer innovation requires companies to continuously rethink whether old recipes still apply. Innovation is triggered by their constant exposure to new market information and ever changing customer demands. They do not limit themselves to incremental adaptations, however: equally important is the search for disruptive change. Often this leads to new business models.

Collaborate

Third, these organizations collaborate with others where their own capabilities fall short. In doing so, they develop the ecosystem required to build and deliver the solutions their customers need. Instead of relying on their own R&D, they stand on the shoulders of suppliers and partners to reach further. They understand that you must work together in order to transform a good idea into a market success.

They orchestrate the activities of an array of partners so that their joint efforts enable new products and solutions for customers. They cleverly exploit their own strengths so they can play a valuable role in the ecosystem they build.

These connect-convert-collaborate processes represent the key capabilities for customer innovation. All three processes are intrinsically linked and lose their individual value when not exercised at the same time.

The strategic case for customer understanding and market insight

Are market-driven companies more innovative than others? Popular voices claim that listening to the customer is detrimental to innovation. The Henry Ford statement, 'If I would have asked my customers what they wanted, they would have said a faster horse' is likely to be quoted in defence of this argument.[1] Leaving the validity of this claim aside, it's interesting to ask whether it's worth being market-driven. Does this lead to better company performance? The answer is an unequivocal yes. Market-oriented firms do better than others on measures such as growth, market share and profitability. But there is one big caveat: market orientation leads to performance, only if it first results in innovation.[2] Picking up market signals when you have no intention of changing course as a result of what you learn is a waste of time. There is no point in investing in customer-centricity when one does not have the mechanisms in place to do something with the insights gained.

Organizations must learn how to drive innovation from both the technology side and the customer side. Sure, a technological discovery can often be leveraged to meet a customer need that before could not be addressed. But, conversely, an unmet customer need can inspire a new technical solution. So the challenge for companies is how to get better at bringing those two sides together. The essence of customer innovation is that the organization and its ecosystem are a united force in addressing a market demand.

Putting the customer first is not a mantra reserved only for those managing customer service. It's not a responsibility only for those on the front line dealing directly with customers; there is a great risk in taking this view. Outside-in organizations do not investigate the unmet needs customers have concerning their products. They are not so much interested in the product features that are missing as in wanting to understand what it really is that customers want to accomplish through the product. Are busy working parent families buying an iPad to enjoy the productivity features and apps it contains? Or are they hiring a convenient on-call babysitter? Do parents take their children to Disneyland to be entertained or do they want to feel connected to and appreciated by their children in spite of their busy lives?

When seeking to understand the underlying function the product fulfils, the next question is: how could this job be accomplished better? This requires organizations to consistently question their existing business model to understand if it still adequately addresses customer needs. The development of this market insights capability is not relegated to a support function, but is seen as a strategic core responsibility that mobilizes every employee.

When we start seeing our products and services through the lens of the real role they fulfil for our customers, we can start seeing the actual solution they provide. As a result of this customer focus, customer innovation organizations operate according to a reversed value chain. Whereas the traditional value chain model regards the market as the end-outcome of the efforts of the organization, the reversed value chain model starts there; see Figure I.2. The customer is the starting point and the value chain is the result of understanding customer needs and requirements.

The antecedents

The shifts we describe are not coincidental; they are intrinsically linked to each other. The steps of moving towards customer innovation are complemented, stimulated and reinforced by three crucial

FIGURE I.2 The reverse value chain

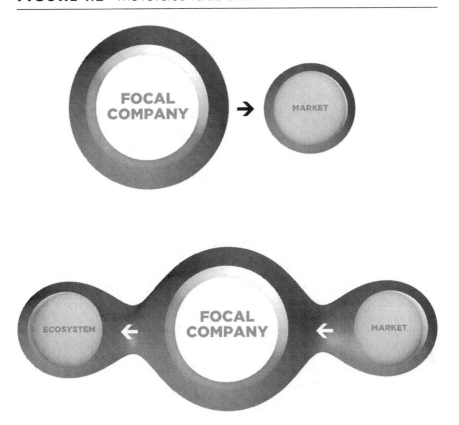

shifts in today's businesses: from a transaction-based to a co-creation-based customer relationship; from a product-oriented to a solutions-oriented focus; and from closed innovation processes to open innovation ecosystems.

First, the expectations of informed and connected people have transformed the extent of engagement they expect from companies: 2010 and beyond has been called the age of the customer.[3] When every product has become commoditized, every technology quickly copied and every customer service gaffe immediately spread on social media, customers increasingly are in the driving seat. The only competitive advantage remaining is a customer advantage,[4] and this customer advantage is increasingly being co-created with customers, employees, managers and other company stakeholders.[5]

Second, the concept of 'solutions' is high on many company agendas. By flawlessly integrating products and services, hence offering added value to its customers, a solution provider is able to beat the commoditization that increasingly threatens both product and service providers. The business imperative for providing solutions is clear. Compared to products, solutions are less easy to copy, offer higher revenue-perspectives, and increase customers' switching costs. From a customer's perspective, solutions directly address the problem that he or she is trying to solve, or the task he or she is trying to carry out. While products may do part of the job, solutions reduce costs and risks for the customer, while getting the job done more effectively.

Third, the concept of open innovation has buried the old innovation paradigm that companies need to rely on their own innovation efforts in order to benefit from them.[6] Instead, over the last decade more and more companies have become convinced that they need to open up their innovation processes and rely on external ideas as much as on internal ones. The compelling reasons to open up the internal R&D centre include faster development and access to new technological developments and new knowledge. The point that we want to take forward is that only by complementing their own set of skills and competences with those of their other partners will organizations be able to bring new customer solutions to the market.

The themes this book addresses are thus not entirely new. Customer-centricity is one of the popular management themes du jour. Making the transition from products to solutions is an endeavour many companies are facing, and 'open innovation' is the latest buzzword in the innovation world. The rationale behind these phenomena is solid and each of these practices is valuable up to a point; that point is reached when one fails to realize that these are not stand-alone trends. The company that innovates around the customer succeeds at combining them to yield the optimal result. The outside-in organization recognizes that each of these practices complement one another and that the full potential of each can only be exploited when they are not seen as silo concepts.

Desperately seeking

Most companies currently face testing times. While the economic downturn threatens the growth of a lot of businesses, other factors have also emerged that have contributed to this situation of the 'perfect storm'. Increased price competition from the traditional low-labour countries coupled with improved product quality from these countries; increasingly demanding customers; advances in technology and information making it easier for the customer to shop around; increased costs of raw materials, and so on, have meant that firms have to look for ways to weather this storm, so that they can survive to fight another day.

In these trying times, organizations are increasingly focusing internally to try to refocus on their core activities/competences and scrutinizing all the other activities that are considered as peripheral and hence do not necessarily add value to the firm[7] – they buckle down, reduce investments in 'nice to have' projects and drive down hard on operational efficiencies. While this act of introspection has led to an 'extensive trimming' of the fat, it does not solve the fundamental problem of commoditization and competition. At best, it allows firms to embrace the low-end rather than escape it.

A second often-trotted road leads firms to search for revenue growth by adding services to their product line. Sales people are trained to become 'solution sellers'. They push complementary products and services onto the market. By adding consultative, advisory, diagnostic and operational services, they seek adjacent business opportunities that surround their core offering. However, the core products are still seen as the locomotive and services as only the derivatives. But as customers carefully vet their needs and watch budgets, pruning all unnecessary expenses, they often resist being compelled to spend further on auxiliary services. This often leads to disappointment in the extent to which these services are able to add significant business. The concept of what it entails to be a real customer-focused solution provider is still misunderstood.

A third popular answer comes from innovation. The bookshops are full of advice for companies to drastically change course and embrace the innovation paradigm. Companies that buy into the innovation imperative appoint Chief Innovation Officers who set up incubation initiatives, and invest in new business models. The innovation champions that lead these initiatives risk being seen as lone rangers, shooting in all directions. Their haphazard attempts at innovation fail to deliver a significant change in the company's culture. Isolated innovation initiatives fail to change the course of the organization they belong to, and instead risk being suffocated by it.

In this book we offer an alternative perspective. What happens when you start viewing everything through the eyes of your customer, when you view the entire customer experience, even when not all of it is controlled by you? When you think beyond the product to the task the customer is trying to solve? When you look at this task through the lens of what it requires to accomplish it, irrespective of your own capabilities? When you start thinking beyond your own organization's boundaries, to the set of parties that may need to collaborate to fulfil the customer's requirements? When you grasp every opportunity to obtain information about your customers in order to better understand them? When you involve customers every step of the way to obtain continuous feedback on how to serve them better?

Focus on the user and all else will follow. Google

Firm-centric paradigm versus customer-centred perspective

A small personal anecdote. I was teaching an introductory class on strategic marketing for an executive MBA group. The group, a good 40 smart managers from international companies, listened attentively. I talked them through an example of a company that had broadened its product portfolio after it discovered that its cash-cow product was not ideal for a part of its potential market. I talked about how it discovered a new segment of customers that could be served better; how it had tried to accommodate all the customer needs and how it had designed the product specifically with this segment in mind.

Then one participant raised his hand and said: 'That's all very nice and fine to listen to. But let's face it, it is much more common to just develop the product first and then find a target group to fit the product rather than do it the other way around. So how do you do marketing in that case, which is much more close to reality?'

The question astounded me at first. And it astounded me even more to see the other nodding heads, and to hear others jumping in, adding that they recognized the 'develop first, then find customer' much more than my 'find customer first, then develop' scenario.

Today, we are 60 years on from the emergence of the marketing concept, yet many organizations are still a long way from having fully developed the market-based point of view. After decades of singing the gospel of the value of customer-centricity, the reality is still very far removed from the ideal. Many organizations still struggle to shake the product-centricity that prevents them from seeing their offering through the customers' eyes, and proactively responding to market needs.

CASE STUDY

Take for example the gigantic blunder Pfizer made in its attempt to revolutionize diabetes care. Pfizer had struck a deal with Nektar Therapeutics, which had developed a radically new technology that would enable patients to inhale their insulin instead of having to inject themselves. Expectations were high for Exubera, the new inhalable insulin offering: as high as $2 billion a year in sales. Analysts expected Exubera to spawn copycats, turning inhaled insulin into a $5 billion annual market.[8] But soon after the launch, Pfizer announced it was pulling the plug on Exubera, returning all rights to Nektar. This was a dramatic reversal of fortune, as a result of a massive miscalculation of customers' wishes and demands. Total cost? A staggering $2.8 billion charge.

What went wrong? In short, Pfizer never fully understood how patients with diabetes manage their disease. What initially attracted the company to Nektar's invention was the idea that inhaled insulin would offer an attractive alternative to patients afraid to stick themselves with needles multiple times a day. But the needle sticks really aren't that much of a hassle, many patients report, and the needles themselves are so thin that they cause virtually no pain. The signals of failure had been on the horizon, but executives chose to ignore them. Even before Pfizer introduced Exubera in mid-2006, patients were blasting it on blogs and online discussion groups for people with diabetes. Patients were not elated to have a daily cumbersome ritual made more convenient. They in fact felt that Exubera was considerably more cumbersome. When folded out for use, it was about the size of a can of tennis balls, not something that could be used discreetly at a restaurant or party. Its dosage could not be adjusted as easily as injected insulin could, and it carried the risk of lung problems. As a result, the few patients who did try Exubera had to endure lung-function tests before they started their new regimen. Ultimately, the patients just gave up. They preferred injected insulin.

The example of Pfizer shows how even capable, big companies can make huge mistakes when it comes to reading customer preferences. In spite of the signal of imminent doom, Pfizer remained blind to the bad news. And when people hear the story of Pfizer, they cannot believe how it is possible to make such an enormous error by remaining blind to customers' problems with the new product. Harvard professor John Gourville explains the driving force behind such miscalculations. Companies tend to overvalue the benefits of their new products by a factor of 3, while customers tend to under-weigh the benefits by a factor of 3.[9] This estimation represents the blind love that we bestow on our own products, and the scepticism on the customers' side. As a result of the 'curse of knowledge', developers expect customers to see the same value in new products as they themselves see. So we push through, and are astonished when instead of overwhelming market success we are met with indifference.

Innovation leaders are often seen as visionaries: people with the capacity to know what we want before we know it ourselves. Steve

Jobs is the poster child of this type of innovation leader. He famously retorted, 'What market research?' when asked about the consumer research that would underpin the iPad development. A second archetype of innovation leader is the maverick: the internal product champion who pushes an innovation through by sheer force of will and, indeed, against the gravitational force of resistance to change. An innovation champion requires perseverance, patience and an unwavering belief in the cause.

As a result of these two innovation leader archetypes, we have come to associate innovation with vision, perseverance and a general aversion to asking customers what they want. Few people will ever question whether there is value for an organization in being customer-oriented, but when it comes to the question whether an organization should listen to its customers when developing new products, we suddenly change our point of view. The prejudice against involving the customers' voice in the innovation process is quite persistent. However, even Steve Jobs could be wrong. The man believed to have a built-in innovation radar also did not have a 100 per cent success rate. For example, Jobs enthusiastically endorsed the Segway, calling it 'the most significant development since the personal computer'. Nevertheless, the Segway never delivered on the initial sales expectations.

The myopic approach to new product development often leads to what we call 'the better mousetrap': a better product that nobody really is waiting for. When product development is not driven by customer needs, it is either driven by technological opportunities or by the eagerness to surpass competitors in product functionality. Both approaches result in products that have to fight 'feature fatigue'.[10] Engineers often find it irresistible to tack on features that lead to novelty value, but daze and confuse ordinary users. Feature overload makes customers yearn for simple products that just do the job they are required to do and nothing more.

Today, we have strong evidence that firms that drive innovation from the market side perform better than average on metrics like growth, market share and profitability. These companies are convinced that if you want to win a game of darts, you better not play blindfolded: if you want to hit the innovation jackpot, you better know where the bull's-eye is. Firms that have adopted a market-centric approach to innovation listen to the signals coming from the market and drive innovation from there. They react to manifest needs of their existing customers, but also anticipate new demands coming from emerging segments. To do this successfully, they deploy three different lenses (see Figure I.3):

1 The first lens is focused on existing customers. By tightening the bonds with their customer base, companies make sure there is a continuous feedback loop that allows them to stay tuned to changing demands and generate the most innovation value out of their customers.

2 The second lens zooms out from the current product range to the entire customer journey. Instead of trying to understand needs concerning their own products, customer innovation companies are more interested in the entire path customers are taking to accomplish a certain outcome that the product helps them to realize.

FIGURE I.3 The three lenses

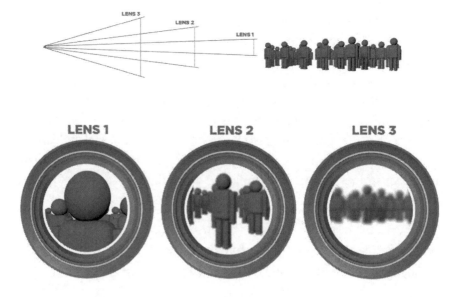

3 Using the third lens, companies zoom out even more to capture the signals from emerging change in the periphery of the market.

For example, if you're an airline, using the three lenses you are focused on three different questions:

Lens 1: What do existing customers expect from us? Should we offer Wi-Fi on the plane?

Lens 2: How can we improve the entire travel experience for customers, from the moment they book a ticket to the moment they step out of their door and until they arrive at their destination?

Lens 3: Will new meeting technology replace business travel?

Using the three lenses enables an organization to have a balanced approach: from creating close connections to current customers to preparing for new markets or market disruptions. Using the three lenses means that we balance current success with future longevity.

The remainder of this book is structured around three building blocks. In each of these blocks, we develop in more depth what it means to deploy each of the three lenses, and how the firm can implement them. We provide illustrations on each, and delineate the role each of the three lenses play. We also show how all three lenses are needed, and how a company deploying only one develops an incomplete view of the market. We demonstrate that being a market-driven organization is not the sole responsibility of innovation leaders but an organization-wide responsibility to be like a sponge that absorbs customer information.

As a result of customer focus, customer innovation operates according to a reversed value chain. Whereas the traditional value chain model regards the market as the end-outcome of the efforts of the organization, the reversed value chain model starts there. The customer is the starting point and the value chain is the result of understanding customer needs and requirements. The configuration of the firm is adapted to best capture customer insights, and (co-)create customer value. Customers dictate how the firm organizes itself to best create the solutions they require.

How to read this book

There are a number of different ways to navigate through this book. Of course, the recommended way is to read it from beginning to end. This way, the text will guide you through the three different steps of the customer innovation process (connect-convert-collaborate) as deployed within each of the three lenses. The nine main chapters together delineate the core areas an organization needs to work on. Chapters 1 to 3 cover the first lens, Chapters 4 to 6 the second, and Chapters 7 to 9 the third lens. Each cluster of three chapters covers, in order, the connect, convert and collaborate steps, and every chapter contains examples and extensive case studies. Each chapter concludes with a short recap and a to-do list on how to get started to implement the ideas in this chapter.

Another way to read the book is to focus on each of the three steps of the connect-convert-collaborate separately:

- If you're most interested in understanding how to better connect with customers you can focus on the first step. By reading Chapters 1, 4 then 7, you get a good sense of how an organization can connect with its customers and market by deploying each of the three lenses.

- If you want to know more about how to convert market and customer insights into innovations, read Chapters 2, 5 then 8. That way you can clearly see how the step of converting differs in each of the three lenses.

- If you want to know what kind of collaborations can help you best to foster market-driven innovation, read Chapters 3, 6 then 9. Each of these three chapters discusses the type of collaborative engagements you need in each lens.

The last chapter of this book shows the interactions between the different parts and presents an overall playbook for customer innovation.

Small ideas with big impact

Rome wasn't built in one day. Implementing customer innovation can be a huge change project. If you feel like you are still far removed from the ideal, don't think you are about to embark on climbing Mount Everest. To set the change in motion, small success projects are needed that create positive energy in the organization. Throughout this book, these ideas are highlighted by a light bulb icon. These so-called 'small ideas with big impact' are meant to show how to get started. They illustrate very concrete practices that companies undertake to support the connect-convert-collaborate process.

However, the intention is not that these ideas should be copied blindly. Individual actions often don't work in isolation: they require the appropriate context and alignment with other initiatives, otherwise there is a risk of counterproductive results and discouraging the troops. For example, many companies copied the widely known practice of 3M to give employees 20 per cent of their time to work on their own pet projects in complete freedom. In spite of this, they failed to reach the same innovation output as 3M. Without the supporting innovation culture, the empowerment from the top, and the breeding ground for new ideas to grow, such isolated initiatives are useless.

In strategy implementation, the devil is often in the detail. A strategy gets implemented by making clear decisions but also creating rituals, practices and communication tools. The 'small ideas with big impact' are meant to inspire and to give ideas on how to turn strategy into practice.

Notes

1 The argument also often seems to be used to avoid the hard work of testing ideas against the market and facing reality.

2 Han, J K *et al* (1998) Market orientation and organizational performance: is innovation a missing link? *Journal of Marketing*, 62, 30–45

3 *Competitive Strategy in the Age of the Customer,* by Josh Bernoff for CMO & Marketing Leadership Professionals, 6 June 2011

4 Joachimstahler, E (2007) *Hidden in Plain Sight,* Harvard Business Review Press, Boston, MA

5 Ramaswamy, V and Gouillart, F (2010) *The Power of Co-creation,* Free Press, New York

6 Chesbrough, H (2030) *Open Innovation,* Harvard Business School Press, Boston, MA

7 Gulati, R and Kletter, D (2005) Shrinking core, expanding periphery: the relational architecture of high-performing organizations, *California Management Review*, 47, 3, spring, 77–104

8 *Business Week,* 18 October 2007

9 Gourville, J (2006) Eager seller and stony buyers, *Harvard Business Review,* June

10 Rust, R *et al* (2006) Defeating feature fatigue, *Harvard Business Review,* February

Connect using the first lens

01

Zooming into the customer: five practices

"You can observe a lot by just watching. **YOGI BERRA**

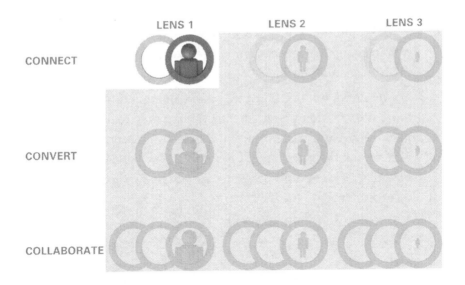

T he first lens contains the narrowest but most in-depth view. It's where we zoom into the company's current customer base with intense focus. The first step of the connect-convert-collaborate process is connecting with customers, geared towards developing rich customer insights. As important as this process may be, it is still a process that companies struggle with. For example, in a recent survey, 63 per cent of CMOs admitted that they needed better capabilities in developing voice-of-the-customer insights.[1]

In the following sections we present five different practices that can help you to engage better with your customer base to get the maximum insights:

1 *Open the channels of conversation.* The first practice is about enabling a constant feedback loop from customers. With this, the company enables a dialogue between customers and the company that allows it to listen to their input on a continuous basis and immediately integrate what is learnt.

2 *Immersive customer understanding.* Immersive customer understanding is about getting close to customers within their own environment. The strongest insights often do not come from studying survey reports about customers, but from understanding the real-life situations of customers. It's only when we immerse ourselves in our customers that we uncover rich insights that reflect their context: their business, their processes, and their life.

3 *Using all the information you have.* Companies often have more information about customers than they realize. The key is to discover all current (and potential) sources of information and unlock their potential. Often, this also means creating new platforms and processes to generate new sources of information.

4 *Customers as a source of ideas.* The best way to make sure that customers have a voice in the company's strategy and actions is to use their ideas to shape your own. Here, we involve customers in the idea-generating process directly.

5 *Customers as developers.* Customers often create solutions for their problems, or adapt products to better suit their needs. In essence, this means that customers take up the role of developers. Smart companies tap into the opportunity to use these ideas and engage customers as developers.

Below we go deeper into each of these practices, explore what they entail and how companies deploy them.

Open up the channels of communication

Outside-in organizations are customer obsessed in that they are constantly looking for ways to learn about their customers. They develop a constant feedback loop with customers, which encourages them to share their comments and experiences so that the company can build customer feedback into its daily operations and continuous improvement efforts. What a company learns through the constant feedback loop focuses the entire organization on meeting customer needs and providing a superior customer experience.[2] Ultimately, it gives direction to the company's strategy and priorities.

The first step is to open up the channel of communication with customers. This involves soliciting feedback (through surveys or interviews) and collecting unsolicited feedback from customers, including monitoring channels you do not own yourself. Customers constantly provide unsolicited and honest feedback through e-mails, service calls, posts on social media, etc. Sometimes they direct that feedback directly to the company, using the channels that the company makes available, but they often do not directly contact the company. They may provide a reference for a colleague, vent their irritation on Twitter, etc.

You need to make sure there is a way for customers to easily pass on their feedback to the company. The goal is to encourage and foster customer feedback rather than trying to minimize it. Lowering the threshold means opening the gates of communication and making it convenient. Outside-in organizations use every channel possible to capture the feedback from customers. They actively solicit feedback and work to remove barriers for spontaneous feedback, instead of trying to limit the extent of engagement. By using multiple channels they create more opportunities for customers to interact with the company. That interaction in and of itself already has immediate benefits for the company. For example, research has uncovered empirical proof that customer engagement and participation in online inter-action about a brand successfully drive immediate sales. The mere fact that somebody said something about you increases that person's likelihood of buying from you.[3]

A first opportunity to learn from customers is by exploring the spontaneous feedback they give through the channels that the company provides such as customer service calls, complaint e-mails, etc. Many companies have worked on automating the conversation with customers in an effort to reduce the costs of customer service. However, if you redirect customers to low-cost channels for questions, complaints and comments, it is often to low-engagement channels. In the long term, this may limit the quality of interactions you have with customers.

CASE STUDY

Customer service king Zappos provides a good illustration of how to gain value from fostering direct customer interactions. The online shoe retailer is renowned for its focus on customer service and its legions of loyal fans as a result. CEO Tony Hsieh sees the people manning the call centre as an important tool to open up the conversation with customers. Instead of automated menus, real-life customer loyalty representatives are available *24 hours a day, 365 days a year* to answer customer questions – *no matter how long they take.*

Instead of hiding its free phone number somewhere in small font on its webpages, it makes sure it is easy for customers to call by prominently showing it on the front page. Call centre representatives do not work with standard scripts, but are trained to engage in a genuine conversation with customers. Customers are encouraged to call the company, because Tony Hsieh believes it to be a great opportunity to develop a personal connection with the customer.[4] The telephone is seen as a unique communication channel, where you have the undivided attention of the customer: rare in a world of information overload. Notoriously, the online shoe and apparel retailer broke its personal record for longest customer service phone call on 8 December 2012 with a conversation that lasted 10 hours and 29 minutes. A member of Zappos' customer loyalty team was apparently just following protocol when he or she took the record-setting phone call. For Zappos, the lengthy conversation is proof of the company's dedication to its customers.

Jeffrey Lewis, Zappos' customer loyalty team supervisor, said: 'Zappos's first core value is deliver wow through service, and we feel that allowing our team members the ability to stay on the phone with a customer for as long as they need is a crucial means of fulfilling this value.'[5] As stories like this are shared across the globe, Zappos's reputation for being a customer-friendly service leader is only solidified.

Smart companies not only monitor what customers tell them directly, but also what they say indirectly about them on other channels that are not controlled by the company. This is what customers say about you, but not to you. Often this happens on social media. Social media monitoring therefore is an essential tool for capturing the conversations that are going on about you, even when your company is not directly involved in the interaction.

In addition to creating easily accessible channels to foster spontaneous feedback, companies also need to actively solicit the feedback. The purpose is to constantly gauge the temperature of your customers' feelings on how you perform. Whether using a metric like customer satisfaction or the Net Promoter Score,[6] the purpose is to get customers to provide their assessment of how well the company is performing on delivering upon customer expectations. Companies can do this on a regular basis for a representative sample of customers, or they can choose to measure customer satisfaction for all customers, at every touch-point. Both approaches are valid, but serve a different purpose. However, as discussed in the next chapter in the section 'Close the feedback loop', care should be taken not to alienate customers.

The first approach involves a once-a-year check-up on customer satisfaction. As such, it supports strategy development and prioritizes product and process improvements based on customer feedback. This approach is useful to gauge how you are doing and to guide decisions and priorities to work on for the future. It can also be used to benchmark with competitors. The downside is that it does not provide the constant pulse of customers. It does not allow an immediate and direct interaction, but is an impersonal approach.

The second approach involves a constant measurement, asking customers for their assessment at every occasion they get in touch with you. For example, Kinepolis, the European cinema group, asks customers after every online ticket purchase what they thought of the film, the service, the experience, etc. Making this measurement part of the regular interaction with customers allows you to have a constant idea of how you are performing. It also allows for feeding the assessment back to service and frontline employees and gives them an accurate view on the customers they were responsible for serving. For example, at Carglass, the employees at every location get a weekly report card for the customers who passed through their location that week.

Tracking this constant pulse has two main advantages. First, it allows you to communicate the results continuously, creating a culture where everybody understands the importance of customers. Second, it allows you to carry out service recovery. The goal of any recovery response is to fix the immediate problem and restore a potentially damaged customer-company relationship. If the customer gave a negative evaluation, you take immediate action to solve this customer's issue, to apologize or to rectify the situation. In other words, it means that you act on the input directly and towards the customer.

TABLE 1.1   The multiple channels of communication with customers

	Solicited	Unsolicited/ spontaneous
Directed at the company		
Not directed at the company		

Learn the language of the customer
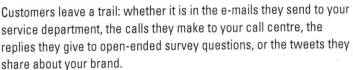

Customers leave a trail: whether it is in the e-mails they send to your service department, the calls they make to your call centre, the replies they give to open-ended survey questions, or the tweets they share about your brand.

By analysing what they write or say we can learn a lot about how customers word things: what are the exact phrases, terminology and words they use? Most likely they do not talk your own lingo, and this analysis can help you to transform your own communication and really talk the customer's language. This can be used again in marketing messages and copy.

Everybody in the organization should listen in to at least three customer calls every week. Doing this serves many purposes:

- It is a signal of the importance of customers.

- It is a constant reminder of who we're working for.

- It is a great source of inspiration.

There is no substitute for the raw and direct contact with customers, and removes the distance that creeps in when you only read about customers in polished summary reports.

Immersive customer understanding

Here's a joke my children like to tell each other. A rabbit enters a bakery and asks the baker: 'Do you have carrot cake?' The baker answers: 'No, unfortunately, I do not have any carrot cake.' The next day, the rabbit comes back, and again asks the baker: 'Do you have any carrot cake?' Again, the baker has to answer: 'No, I'm afraid I do not have any carrot cake.' Later that day the baker decides that he will start adding carrot cake to his standard assortment. That way, he can finally offer the poor rabbit a carrot cake and make him happy. So when the next day the rabbit returns, and asks: 'Do you have any carrot cake?', the baker proudly answers: 'Yes indeed, I do have some carrot cake.' Upon which the rabbit says: 'It's horrible isn't it?'

As silly as this story is, it can be eerily close to the real-life experience of meeting customer demands. Thousands of new products are launched each year. But over 90 per cent of them fail – and it's not always because of a lack of attention in trying to understand what customers want. Companies attempt to listen to customer requests, only to be turned down when they launch onto the market and customers have already moved on. When they fail to see the results they hoped for, executives scratch their heads and conclude that customers don't really know what they want. But ultimately we have no choice but to listen to the market: it is always the market that is the ultimate judge of our products and services.

But what people say in surveys can be highly unreliable. They may claim they would purchase a product, but get cold feet when it comes to actually doing so.[7] Besides, people are notoriously bad at predicting upfront what features they are actually going to use. Ex-ante they are optimistic about the usefulness of new features, but when they are available to them, they do not actually use them.[8] The newer the product, the bigger the gap between pre-launch intentions and post-launch purchase and usage behaviour. When there is an existing product category to refer to, and customers are experienced users, there is also the danger that one only comes up with copycat features from competing products. As a result, the company just converges to the mean, but risks never really differentiating from existing offerings in the market.[9]

The culprit lies in how we try to understand customers. Given the quantitative nature of today's business, and the desire to be able to back up a business case with solid numbers, we often quickly jump to quantitative surveys to validate our assumptions. But the customer is not a study object, to be researched on your own terms in surveys, focus groups and online questionnaires. You will not necessarily find the answers you are looking for by surveying the customer to death. You can drown yourself in data, but do you really have insight? To gather real insight, you need to get out from behind your desk and into the field, getting your hands dirty. Surveys can be a useful tool to gather customer feedback about specific interactions and about situations and products customers are very familiar with. Surveys can also be useful to get a quantitative validation that gives statistical relevance to preliminary conclusions. But surveys are entirely the wrong tool to discover the 'why' behind customers' behaviour, or to uncover the latent needs behind their statements. What about interviews and focus groups then? They might not be able to give you a quantitative view, but surely they are better suited to provide answers to the 'why' questions? Indeed, but it assumes that customers are able to answer the 'why' question.

When it comes to really understanding customer needs, there is no substitute for immersing yourself in their activities by studying them in their own environment. The goal is to investigate the customer in the natural habitat, not through the filter of surveys, questionnaires or interviews. By observing customers in their normal routine, you gain access to information that would otherwise be undetected. You go into the field, behaving like an anthropologist more than a market researcher, not armed with questions and surveys, but with your eyes open, your senses awakened and the question 'why' constantly on your lips.

Ethnography is the branch of anthropology that involves trying to understand how people live their lives. Unlike traditional market researchers, who ask specific, highly practical questions, anthropo-logical researchers visit consumers in their homes or offices to observe and listen in a non-directed way.[10] By understanding how people live or work, researchers discover otherwise elusive trends that inform the company's future strategies. Intel, for example, employs a group of corporate ethnographers that dig into questions such as whether TV and PC technology will converge. Are baby boomers retaining their PC and TV habits as they age, or are they comfortable shifting to new media? Will smartphones take over most of the functions of personal computers? With smartphones, for example, we can con-trast the technology perspectives of teenagers, who have used cell phones since they were in primary school, with those of older genera-tions, who came to them only after becoming proficient with PCs. The job of anthropologists is to understand the perspective of the customer and translate it to convey deep-seated customer insights.

You don't have to go as far as Intel to benefit from observing custom-ers. Within a customer's natural environment, there are often a lot of discoveries that would go undetected otherwise. It makes visible customers' own work-arounds or solutions when products do their job sub-optimally. By using the product in a real-life situation, customers themselves are reminded of issues and obstacles they have, that they might not even think about when prompted in an out-of-context interview. Seeing that overall context may also lead to new opportunities that are adjacent to the core offering.

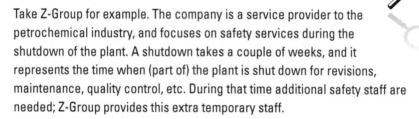

CASE STUDY

Take Z-Group for example. The company is a service provider to the petrochemical industry, and focuses on safety services during the shutdown of the plant. A shutdown takes a couple of weeks, and it represents the time when (part of) the plant is shut down for revisions, maintenance, quality control, etc. During that time additional safety staff are needed; Z-Group provides this extra temporary staff.

When the founder of the fledgling service provider observed what happened during a shutdown at customers' sites, it became apparent that they faced many additional obstacles than he had been aware of. The extra safety staff during the shutdown meant that additional personal safety material and gear was needed and it had to be collected up at the end of the process. Often, it would get lost. These observations led to services beyond providing safety staff: equipment rental, the installation of a track and trace system, on-site vending machines, and temporary localized stock, making Z-Group a total solution provider for all safety-related concerns during the shutdown, instead of a company that only provided one component of the solution to the overall problem customers faced.

Z-Group used the opportunity gathered by observing customers without making it a specific project. It was a natural process as the company was active on the customer's site, performing its services. It discovered opportunities thanks to an entrepreneurial leader with a keen eye and a genuine interest in the customer's business. Obviously, customer observation can also be utilized within well-defined research projects specifically aimed at discovering new opportunities to solve customers' issues.

CASE STUDY

Take the experience of Televic. Televic develops, manufactures and installs top end high-tech communication systems for specific niche markets, such as the healthcare, rail and education sectors. Headquartered in Belgium, it employs about 400 people worldwide. Within its Healthcare division, Televic sells systems for nurse call, intercom, access control, patient entertainment and care registration. Televic's nurse call system offers communication and information to assist the healthcare staff in responding to patients' needs. The company has a strong focus on innovation and technology, but is well aware that technology can only be effective when it is accepted by users.

To support its product development effort, Televic uses observational studies in hospitals. It observes nurses and doctors at work by tagging along, following during their normal routine. By doing this, it fully understands what the doctors and nurses are dealing with while caring for patients, handling administration and the operational processes within the hospital. Without having to ask any questions, product design choices are inspired or ruled out by these observations.

While these observation sessions are very useful, there are not a lot of opportunities to put questions to the hospital staff while on duty – their main focus during a busy work day is on reassuring the quality of care, not fielding the questions of a nosy observational researcher. To handle this challenge, Televic also developed a 'patient room of the future' facility in a dedicated location. This simulated environment looks in every way like a real hospital room. Nurses are invited to participate in sessions where they enact their normal work routines, but where there is more time available to explore in depth what their needs and wishes are. The purpose of such a simulated environment is to create a context that is as close as possible to the real-life situation so that participants are prompted to act like they would do normally, and encounter the typical situations they deal with. That way, they often think about issues that would not come up in an interview away from the work environment.

It is important that insight gained from work like this is shared within the organization and doesn't remain the sole property of a handful of R&D people and product managers. To facilitate internal communication, Televic documents results and insights in a way that is easy to understand and discuss, using user stories and personas, so when somebody is referring to 'this is a product for Malika', everybody right away knows this is a product for a nurse.

There are at least five things we can learn through observation and immersion:[11]

1 *Understanding unarticulated needs.* The greatest benefit to come from observing customers is discovering problems they encounter. By doing this, we make the distinction between manifest and latent demands. Manifest demands are those that customers can easily articulate. Latent demands are more difficult for customers to express, but they are the real reason behind their manifest demands. Getting to the latent demands is based on constantly asking 'why?'

2 *Discover emotional benefits.* Seeing the product being used can evoke a better understanding of the emotional benefits that it triggers. For example, when interviewing a new mother about what she requires from a diaper, she will probably talk about functional benefits such as keeping the baby dry, preventing leakage, convenient closures, etc. But when you see her putting the diaper on, you may see how this is an intimate moment of one-to-one interaction with the baby. You may see her cooing and cuddling, and tickling the baby's tummy. Such is the story behind the growth of the Pampers brand – now

an $8 billion a year business, grown from being 'only' a $2 billion brand a few years ago. Technology and functional benefits had overtaken the consumer as the focus of P&G's efforts. Dryness wasn't the essence for mothers – the baby's development was – and once you define it in those terms, the relevance of the brand and the service becomes totally different.[12] Pampers now provides a service for mothers and babies all around the globe, including information about health, breast-feeding, and so on. Around Christmas time, the Pampers brand works with Unicef, offering a vaccine for a child in need for every packet of Pampers sold. The lesson is that when you are able to define the emotional benefits associated with a product, you can take things further and grow in a whole new way.

3 *Observe user customization.* We can see what kind of adaptations the customers make to our products to tailor them or to adjust them to better suit their particular needs.

4 *See the product in its context.* The Case Study on page 28 about Z-Group highlights the opportunities gained from seeing a product or service in context: it allows you to see complementary products and services (such as when Z-Group realized companies struggled to provide the gear and materials needed for the temporary safety guards). Seeing the product in context also allows you to see potential gains from fitting products and services better with their context (this happened when Z-Group realized that tracking down materials and moving them to the desired location was a hassle for customers). And finally, we might see how we can better streamline products and services where they interface with others.

5 *Understand triggers of use.* Understanding when and why customers use your product can help you understand the role the product plays for your customer, and what are typical triggers for use. The phrase 'Have a break, have a Kit-Kat' captures this idea of understanding triggers for use.

Using every source of information you have

Remember the tale of Hansel and Gretel and how they followed their trail of pebbles to find their way back home? Just like Hansel threw pebbles along the way, customers very often leave traces behind. Following these traces will tell us where our customers are. Customers leave traces as they search for information, use products and services and share experiences with their peers. These traces are nuggets of information that reveal patterns of behaviour, tacit needs and systems of interrelated activities that customers undertake. Piecing these traces together and aggregating data from multiple sources creates a unique understanding of the market and enables companies to uncover real needs behind expressed demand, as well as opportunities that are untapped and often implicit.[13] But just as the pebbles looked innocuous in the woods, we often do not even realize the potential of the information we have.

Most businesses gather considerable amounts of data about the customers that buy from them. And despite significant progress in analytical capabilities and technological tools, those data remain remarkably underutilized. Most companies have only scratched the surface of the possibilities they could exploit if they could transform their information into knowledge and usable intelligence. Modern technology, the internet and the digitization of consumers' lives have created an environment awash in data. Each type of data has the potential to paint a picture for better customer understanding, and can offer unique insights that cannot be obtained otherwise. If we are able to see the big picture behind the individual data points, we transform data into insight. This broad view across customers contains value that can be leveraged to create new products, services, knowledge, value and competitive advantage.

The challenge for businesses is to recognize their unique ability to piece together information puzzles and to identify untapped customer insights. A customer base may contain thousands, even millions of customers. Each customer carries a piece of the puzzle. If collected and aggregated, these pieces will reveal patterns. The resulting trends can uncover underlying causes of purchase behaviour, patterns and commonalities in behaviour, and may even reveal needs, previously unseen.

CASE STUDY

Take for example, one of the latest inventions of Coca-Cola. It is not yet a new soda or beverage, but transforms the customer experience of choosing and ordering a drink. Coca-Cola Freestyle is a style of soda fountain. The Coca-Cola Freestyle soda dispenser turns the entire drink experience into one where the consumer is in complete control. Whereas traditional soda fountains are limited in the range they can provide, this new machine can offer consumers a choice of 125 different drinks. Instead of using five-gallon boxes of syrup as in traditional fountains, Freestyle employs cartridges filled with various flavours, much like modern printers hold and dispense different-coloured ink. Micro-dosing technology from the medical industry allows precise amounts to be dispensed to meet Coca-Cola flavour standards.

While consumers are interacting with the high-tech push-button screen and enjoying the fun experience of selecting their personal choice, various types of software applications are measuring what was purchased in what quantity at what time in what location. Each night, the machines transmit detailed data to Coca-Cola on what brands sold and when. Already, they've discovered that the popularity of Caffeine-Free Diet Coke spikes after 3 pm. Beaming all that info back helps to understand in far greater detail real-life consumption patterns that can never be detected in consumer surveys.

With customer transaction and purchase information like the data Coca-Cola is able to collect, it is obvious to most people that this can be usefully leveraged by the company. The $18 billion CRM market demonstrates this clearly. Customer transaction data are widely available in many industries such as e-commerce, financial services, utilities, telecoms, etc. These industries thus have a long tradition of crunching the numbers to understand individual customers' value as well as predicting future potential sales and cross-selling potential. If transactional data are not available, customer loyalty cards and loyalty programmes are used to generate them. Not only do these loyalty programmes incentivize customers to purchase more from one company, they also incentivize customers to have their purchases tracked.

CASE STUDY

Start-up company Quidsi has leveraged this ability fully. In 2005, the company started the online retailer Diapers.com, selling all the necessities a new mum and dad require. From the start, it used purchase data to build proprietary models to help them understand the typical purchase patterns of customers with different profiles. Using location, demographic and purchase information, it is now able to profile customers with a remarkable accuracy. From the first purchase a consumer makes, it can predict the entire revenue this customer will generate in the future.[14] The more purchases and corresponding data it collects, the more accurate the algorithm becomes, building a real competitive advantage. This competitive advantage led to a company that after four years generated £180 million in revenue and was acquired by Amazon in an estimated $540 million deal. Companies that have not yet explored the goldmine of customer purchase data are clearly losing out and falling behind.

There are additional steps to be taken that go beyond purchase data, customer demographics and the goal of predicting the next transaction. The first step is to uncover hidden sources of information that remain unexplored. Often, just like Hansel and Gretel, customers leave behind traces that we are not aware of. Our job is to find out the tracks they leave behind, and use them to generate insights.

When there are no available sources, companies work to generate new possibilities to gather information about customers.

CASE STUDY

In mid-2012, Disneyworld introduced a new holiday management system for the visitors at its theme parks. On arrival, visitors to the Disney parks in Orlando are given an electronic bracelet that not only contains their credit card data but also acts as a room key and a theme-park ticket. Guests can enter their favourite attractions and are invited to try them when they are not so busy. The objective is to enhance the customer experience. Cinderella can greet your children by name because the magic bracelet displays the info as you approach her. And if it happens to be your birthday, the theme park characters will congratulate you. Apart from a service upgrade, the bracelet also offers other advantages. Buying products and having them delivered to your room is easy and quick. Until now, this came with a lot of administrative formalities for both guests and staff. Now, thanks to MyMagic+, the process is now fully automatic.

Obviously Disney is also hoping the system will inspire its visitors to spend more.[15] The possibilities for Disney are virtually limitless, but the biggest gain may not be the enhanced customer experience or the efficiency improvements. The biggest gain in the long run is that a new source of information is unlocked; information that previously was virtually impossible to collect. Disney can now trace every step a customer takes through the park. Analysing the patterns and routines of customers can open up endless avenues for data exploration that can lead to new services and enhanced experiences for customers.

So, in conclusion, there are three questions to ask yourself:

1 Are we using the full potential of our customer information already?

2 Are there any hidden sources of information we have never utilized but that are readily available?

3 Can we invent new ways to collect behavioural information about our customers?

Customers as a source of ideas

Are customers equipped with the right knowledge to specify the features they would like to see in a product or service? After all, they are not trained product designers and spend far less time thinking about your products than you do. Giving customers the job of translating their needs into concrete product features may be too much to ask of them. This is especially so where there is no existing product context they are familiar with; this makes it difficult for customers to formulate their wishes. Imagine you are asking somebody who's never seen Google Glass about the main features and attributes they would like to see in the final product. The lack of product experience means that customers lack the language and reference points to articulate their needs. But provided with a frame of reference, customers are very well suited to coming up with new ideas. In fact, their ideas are often more innovative and out-of-the-box than the ideas from specialists within your organization.[16]

Consider the example above of Televic and how it changed its innovation approach. In the past, new ideas would originate from R&D people who never had any customer contact, and would be off to development without a rigorous market testing process. Now, no single idea gets past the first development gate without input from customers. Design workshops, brainstorms and games are used to co-create new ideas and solutions with customers. A specially purchased 3-D printer allows Televic to create real-life rough prototypes, on which customers can give their feedback.

When customers are used as a source of ideas, they are part of the design team and become engaged in making things better. The advantage of involving customers early on in the design process is clear – preventing you from rolling out a mistake on a grand scale:

- The starting point for a co-creation initiative with customers should be the customer's own experience. Instead of creating a frame of reference that is centred on a particular product, frame the context around a task the customer needs to get done, and how he or she goes about it now.

- Do not underestimate the extent to which customers want to contribute voluntarily. Customers are intrinsically motivated to participate. Sometimes, the simple enjoyment of the innovation task itself can be a powerful factor, particularly when what appears to be 'work' is not perceived to be work at all. Exercises that are inherently interesting or intellectually challenging can attract tremendous participation from outsiders, especially when the contributors feel that they are part of some larger cause.[17] So it is important to appeal to this motivation and make the co-creation format fun, challenging and engaging.

- It is advisable to involve employees directly in the co-creation exercise with customers to create buy-in of the new ideas. The direct contact makes all the difference. It promotes buy-in and prevents the 'graveyard' effect: when ideas from outside enter the vetting and evaluation process inside, they are the victim of the not-invented-here syndrome and die a silent death.

- Customers are your best ambassadors. Use your collaborators not just to get ideas from, but also to share within their network about their co-creation experience.

- Customers come with unexpected solutions.[18] While you may think that you can come up with the same things, most people are surprised to find that customers have a different point of view and therefore come up with novel ideas. In fact, companies often suffer from the 'local-search' problem: they search for new ideas and solutions that are close to their existing experience and expertise. This is a block to finding alternative, potentially more successful ideas. Individuals from outside are often in a better position to find innovative solutions because they frame the problem differently.

- Prototypes help you make things tangible, but they should not be finished. Finished prototypes do not give customers a lot of freedom to change or revise things: too much is set in stone already. As a consequence, finished prototypes merely invite criticism, but they do not invite new ideas on how to improve things. An important part of the process is to present customers with concepts that are unfinished and unpolished, but still bring them as close as possible to the real experience.

The points above illustrate the principles of co-creation with customers.[19] When it goes well, customers become part of the new product development team. New products and services are literally co-created.

Recently, the possibilities for customer research have expanded dramatically beyond the classic tools of focus groups, surveys and questionnaires. In particular, the internet has opened up new opportunities to engage with customers on an ongoing basis to get their input and ideas. Companies have started using online platforms to gauge customer needs and insights in a number of different ways. One example is 'idea banks', which are online platforms where customers can leave their ideas and input. Other than voting and sharing, there is often no other interaction between the participants. Participants are invited to post ideas for new products or features without any further specification. Idea banks are mainly used as repositories of new product ideas but they may also reveal some market trends or insights. The advantage of idea banks is that they provide convenient channels for customers to express their wants; Microsoft for example uses them to collect new feature requests. Idea banks however miss out on the potential richness that an online platform can generate. For that, other types of online platforms are more suitable.

A market research online community is a virtual platform on which the company conducts market research activities, such as mini surveys or focus groups, discussions and concept tests. The distinct advantage of a market research online community over regular online market research is that it is possible to overcome the usual reach/richness trade-off. The interactivity of the communication in an online community allows for richness in the discussion. At the same time, it is possible to involve a large number of people[20] for a longer period of time than you could do in a real-life setting such as a focus group. Online communities typically run for a limited time, with a fixed set of recruited participants who fit a desired profile. Heineken used such a community to design the club of the future: 120 design-savvy clubbers participated in a three-week brainstorm, and provided a complete customer journey roadmap.[21] Market research communities like this provide inspiration for new product development or product improvements and can yield concrete solution ideas.

The same could be argued for user groups. A user group can be defined as a virtual group of users, fans and enthusiasts set up to share ideas and experiences with a particular product, often without formal links to the owner company. User groups are generally observed and sometimes even sponsored by product managers of the owner company and are used as a pool for insights related to product use, which may inspire the company to augment some product features. However, in some cases the community actively offers solutions to some problems and unsatisfied market needs they have.

The final type of online community is initiated by the company and provides a continuous platform for exchange with customers. The difference here is that this community has no expiry date. It can be open to everyone, or closed (only upon approval or invitation). Starbucks for example recently celebrated the five-year anniversary of its My Starbucks Idea platform. On this online platform, anyone can share ideas, vote on them and discuss them.

CASE STUDY

Adidas had great success with such a community. The Adidas Insiders started in 2009 on a small scale – locally in the United States – and in 2010 Adidas opened it up to a global audience, recruiting members around the world. Joining the Adidas Insiders happens on invitation only. The criteria for selection are past participation in Adidas initiatives, affinity to sports and age. The company offers no reward in return for joining, as it wants members to join out of interest in being part of the brand. The way Adidas drives motivation and participation within the community is by giving members creative assignments. Any department that wants to get an input or organize an ideation exercise will shoot a short video, in which it is speaking to the community, explaining the problem and asking for their participation. The direct contact with Adidas people proves to be a good technique to motivate member engagement. The members feel that they are working together with real people, not an anonymous organization.

The community is set up in a way that members may be engaged in a plethora of activities. Activity and interaction happens on two levels. The first is when Adidas asks the members to give the company feedback on something. This may happen for each member individually, or Adidas provokes a discussion on certain topics among the members and then the feedback is more of an interactive process. There are also mini-questionnaires the members are asked to complete. There are also more interactive formats like lab chat, where there is an intense discussion with a limited number of people. Small subgroups may be formed in a private setting in the community, to discuss specific subjects with a selected group, like a virtual focus group.

The other level of interaction occurs when members start talking to each other, outside of any initiative from Adidas. Members started setting up their own discussion boards. These are also used by Adidas to gain insights. Spontaneous member engagement is seen as a great way to gather information about the latest trends and also learn the consumer lingo.

The rewards for Adidas, after four years of running the Adidas Insiders, are multiple. Of course the community generates useful customer insights, but that's not the only benefit. First of all, the community is a fast and cost-effective way to engage in market research directly with consumers. Second, the community increases the engagement of its members with the brand and makes them even stronger brand ambassadors.

When setting up a community like the Adidas Insiders, be sure that there is a strong team to support the project within the company.

Reward for contribution

When running an online community, reward participants for their activity rather than for the ideas they bring to the table. Online communities are not contests. The quality and longevity of the interaction they create depends on the collaborative behaviour members exhibit, so the purpose is not to create competition amongst participants. Communities require mechanisms that facilitate and encourage knowledge exchange and interactions among members. The aim is to create a culture of sharing (and learning), a sense of affiliation (as well as identity and status), and perhaps even personal relationships among the participants based on the feeling that you are part of a community of like-minded individuals. To facilitate all of this, the extent of contribution and community-promoting behaviour of participants needs to be rewarded and put in the spotlight.

At Adidas for example, there is the 'Insider of the month' initiative, with the winner getting a goodie bag from Adidas. The participants also get a badge to say that they were the Adidas Insider in a particular month and year. Nominees are chosen by the community, as well as the company. The company makes sure that they advertise whoever their favourite is by creating a story about the person's contribution and posting it onto the community site, showcasing who they voted for. Adidas also highlights the awarded members and in turn members who are awarded usually 'go public', thanking Adidas for the recognition of their efforts.

Some companies integrate gamification in the community. In this system, usually there are points awarded to the members for their activity on the platform. The advantage of this system is that it not only fosters collaboration, but it also indirectly stimulates activity on the platform, as the more activities any given member performs, the more points he or she gets.

Using online customer communities is not only reserved for big consumer brands such as Starbucks and Adidas, which can use their branding power to attract participants. It's also not the exclusive territory of consumer companies, as the example of Eurex demonstrates.

CASE STUDY

Eurex is in the business of selling derivatives in the financial market.
It is a public company wholly owned by Deutsche Börse AG and one of
the world's leading derivatives exchanges. With market participants
connected from 700 locations worldwide, trading volume at Eurex exceeds
1.5 billion contracts a year.

Eurex started to engage in co-creation communities in early 2010 by creating
a virtual environment for its customers. The initial starting point was not to
copy popular social media, but to strengthen the innovation capability of the
company and use every opportunity to communicate with its customers. The
online community was divided into a discussion board and an idea board.
The discussion board serves mainly as a means of socializing and leading
discussions on topics related to trading and the financial world. A typical
member is a bank or an insurance company trader who is well informed about
the financial markets and financial products. Mostly they are experts on the
topic, very much interested in sharing opinions and building their professional
network. The idea board enables customers to submit their ideas. A dedicated
Eurex team will go through the ideas submitted and respond to each of the
authors individually. If an idea is very interesting or needs to be clarified, the
company may transfer the idea to the discussion board and let the community
express their views on it or help to refine it. The project is strengthening the bond
between Eurex and its customers, and is also fostering innovation within the
company by opening up the company culture.

People within organizations are often surprised by the valuable contributions coming from customers they thought they knew well. The
online community that companies create does not replace the long-
established one-to-one relationships with customers, in which conversations about ideas for innovation also take place. But it does
create a new avenue to generate ideas. It creates an opportunity for
customers to discuss things and share ideas with others who have
similar issues. The online community makes it possible to expand
the reach of discussion and the type of issues that can be discussed.
Virtual communities can provide a safe haven of depersonalization,

where a more open approach is possible than might be the case in a face-to-face setting.

Opening yourself up to invite ideas from customers is becoming a necessity and an Olympic minimum. What does it say about you when you do not open yourself up to this channel for customers to engage? Apart from the insights gained, opening up demonstrates a genuine willingness by the company to be open up with its customers and shows it cares. Companies that have started working with customers to generate new product ideas and concepts list the following benefits from investing in the endeavour:

- The input from customers helps to avoid sure-fire failures.
- During development, there are less doubts and discussion on features.
- Less redesign after launch.
- More involvement and motivation from R&D people.
- More involvement from customers, who feel they are being heard. As a consequence they trust the product and are more loyal to the company.
- The co-creation process serves as a pre-launch. The customers who participate already feel involved and have a high likelihood of buying. Those customers who were not directly involved can also be affected, through the word-of-mouth coming from participants.
- Adoption barriers are lower.
- In the short run co-creation slows down the new product development process but in the long run it speeds it up tremendously.

Say thank you!

Participants in co-creation rarely feel being rewarded for their input is important: what they are after is openness and gratitude from the company. They need to feel validated and respected for their contribution and it is very important to take this into account when designing the creative process within a co-creation initiative. Participants should get feedback on the results of the exercise, as well as information on what happened with the selected ideas and insights. They should be validated as having created real value for the company; this way they will see the exercise as meaningful and are likely to participate again.

Some companies invite their partners or customers to submit insights or ideas for innovation that disappear into a 'black box' after submission. They are not visible to the others and not traceable for the author. While this approach will ensure maximum protection of ideas in specific industries, in which an attractive idea could be quickly stolen or misused, it is harmful in the end. The whole idea of co-creation is to foster a natural collaborative ideation process, because it leads to better and richer ideas. Furthermore, if this precaution is necessary, companies should make sure they give feedback on each and every idea to the author submitting it. This may be done virtually in external online communities or even face-to-face in small-scale ones, which yields further advantages.

The important thing is: if you want to keep customers motivated to participate in co-creation initiatives you need to keep them informed and show them gratitude.

Customers as developers

Some of us live in the future today, and some of us will still live in the past tomorrow.

Customer input for idea generation may come in two different forms. The first is geared towards revealing important user needs that are not met by currently available products. This needs-based information (ie, what is the problem?) might then serve as a starting point for a firm's own endeavours to find ways to deal with these unresolved needs (ie, how can we solve the problem?) The second and more controversial type of user input is about solution-based information – asking customers not only about their problems but also about potential ways they can be solved. We often think that customers are well-suited to address the first type of question, but that they're incapable of dealing with the second. The opposite is true. As it turns out, customers are well-equipped to come up with solutions, and they are already doing it to serve their own needs. We just need to uncover this untapped source.

CASE STUDY

In 1893, Josephine Cochrane unveiled an innovation at the Chicago World's Fair: the first truly functional dishwasher. A prominent socialite, she had grown tired of her servants' tendency to break her 17th century fine china and began to wash the dishes herself. She reportedly said: 'If nobody else is going to invent a dishwashing machine, I'll do it myself.' She subsequently formed her own firm, Cochran's Crescent Washing Machine Company, to manufacture the machines, primarily for sale to hotels and restaurants. Cochrane's company eventually became KitchenAid, part of the Whirlpool Corporation.[22]

Customers don't necessarily passively wait for companies to better fit products to their needs: they often take matters into their own hands. In fact, 6 per cent of users create or modify one or more of the products they use in order to address their needs.[23] The collective R&D budget they represent exceeds the corporate R&D budget. They want businesses to pick their ideas up and make them commercially available. But when that doesn't happen, they might just do it themselves.

CASE STUDY

When Phil Baechler became a father, he searched for a way to combine his running habit with the limited time he had as a new dad. He had got into the habit of bringing his son along with him in his baby carriage while jogging. He quickly discovered that standard carriages were not made to endure the stress of long distance usage over various surfaces, so he designed a specialized stroller with features more conducive to running.[24] In 1984, Phil founded Baby Jogger. Today, Baby Jogger continues to be a leading designer and manufacturer of high performance jogging strollers and all-terrain strollers.

Similarly, Baby Einstein was founded in 1994 by Julie Clark, a mum who wanted to share her love of the arts and humanities with her baby. She incorporated classical music and artistic images into a video for her infant. By 2000 the brand was estimated to be worth nearly $400 million in revenues, and was acquired by the Walt Disney Company.

All of these stories illustrate the phenomenon known as 'user innovation'. User innovation is from all eras and is much more prevalent than we think. For example, 43 per cent of key innovations in windsurfing, skateboarding and snowboarding were commercialized by end-users.[25] When it comes to scientific instruments, 77 per cent of the innovations are estimated to come from users;[26] 84 per cent of companies in the category of baby and children's gear were founded by user-entrepreneurs,[27] mums, dads and grandparents who did not find on the market what they were looking for and decided to do something about it. Some products were revolutionary and created entirely new categories, such as Phil Baechler's baby stroller or Josephine Cochrane's dishwasher.

User-innovators experiment and create a novel solution first of all to satisfy their own needs. At this point they usually don't think about turning their invention into a business to profit from the innovation. That idea gets triggered by exposing their innovation to others by using it. Once the innovator begins to use the product/service in public, others see it, often providing feedback and sometimes expressing interest in buying it. This expression of interest frequently sparks the idea of founding a firm.

Clearly, there is a wealth of ideas that have already been developed by customers, waiting to be picked up by companies and brought to the market. Only 2 per cent of these innovating consumers patented their ideas, and many distributed them free of charge.[28] Research on commercial and retail banking services shows that in 85 per cent of these cases, users self-provided the service before any bank offered it.[29] In other words, we just need to be observant enough to notice what our customers are doing, to pick up ideas for new products and services. User innovation from our customers can replace R&D as a source of ideas.

Users have some significant advantages over others for coming up with successful ventures. First, users truly innovate on a needs-basis. The needs they experience may be idiosyncratic, but more often than not they are pretty universal and strike a chord with a larger audience. Because they have a privileged window into both needs and solutions, users can generate creative ideas. Not only do users understand their own needs (what the product is used for), but they also have a distinctive perspective on how it is used, and they automatically integrate this usage aspect in the original idea. Finally, users have a sense of demand from the market feedback they have received either from a community or through their own public use of the innovation.

Increasingly the line between consumers and the companies producing products for them is blurring. Consumers themselves take up the role of inventor and producer. Smart companies don't see this as a threat but join forces with consumer-makers.

What the above tells us is that our approach to driving innovation from customers should not be limited to trying to understand customers and more about unleashing the innovative force that is already present within your customer base. If people have ideas and want to share them, and you do not give them the opportunity to do so, they will go away and you will never know about the idea – or they may take it forward themselves.

Unleash new potential

In this chapter, we propose five different practices that can be used to connect with customers, detect customer insights and enable innovation based on market needs. The full spectrum of practices can be summarized and structured as in the typology matrix in Figure 1.1. The five practices differ in terms of the mode of learning being activated by the company and the purpose. The mode of learning can be passive observation or active solicitation. Passive observation includes observing what innovative users do, customer observation, data tracking and analysis. In essence, in passive observation we find information in what customers are doing already and there is no direct intervention involved. Active solicitation requires the recruitment of participants and involves a direct intervention. The second dimension of the framework highlights the purpose of what you hope to find out. This can be an insight (what is the need?) or go further towards a solution (how can the need be fulfilled?)

The first quadrant contains practices where we actively search for customer insights. The continuous feedback loop with customers fits in this category, as well as immersive customer understanding. Both practices require an active involvement from customers, and they are invited to participate. The purpose of both is mainly to detect unmet customer needs. We also argue that customers can actively be solicited as a source of ideas for concrete solutions on how their needs can better be delivered upon. With this, we have only covered half of the spectrum of the range of possibilities to connect with customers. Passive observation depends on exploiting information that is readily there, and you do not have to bother customers to obtain and use them. Finally, we also discussed how we can tap into the potential of customer-developers as they have developed ready-made solutions for their own needs.

FIGURE 1.1 The matrix of practices

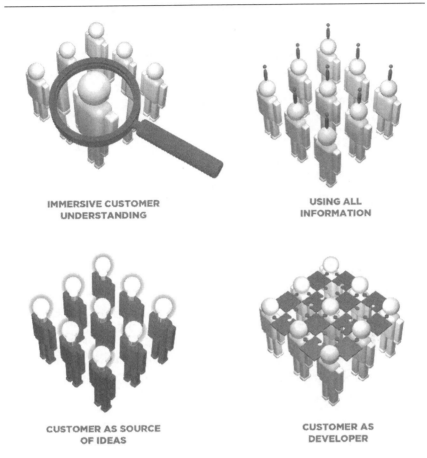

IMMERSIVE CUSTOMER
UNDERSTANDING

USING ALL
INFORMATION

CUSTOMER AS SOURCE
OF IDEAS

CUSTOMER AS
DEVELOPER

In short

- The first step in becoming an outside-in company is developing deep customer connections.
- Relentlessly listen to your customers, searching for new insights.
- Build the processes that enable you to be like a sponge, constantly absorbing information about customers.
- There is a plethora of learning opportunities in the daily interactions with customers.
- Exploit the full spectrum of methods to learn from customers.

- Immerse yourself in your customer's activities. Become the expert in your customer's life or your customer's business.

- Make the customer an active partner in your innovation process. Don't underestimate the willingness and ability of customers to generate ideas.

- A company can create bonds with customers by allowing them 'inside'. Don't see your customers as outsiders to your organization, but as part of it.

Get started

- Invest in enabling a constant feedback loop for customers.

- Create convenient and low-entry channels for customers to communicate with you.

- Don't just ask questions; a lot can be learnt by observing what customers are doing.

- Establish an inventory of the customer information you possess as part of every interaction and touch-point with customers you currently have.

- Create new ways to generate individual customer information that captures (real-time) customer behaviour.

- Get direct access to user experiences by setting up a customer community.

Notes

1 IBM Global CMO study, 2012

2 http://www.netpromotersystem.com/system-processes/closed-loop.aspx

3 Malthouse, E C, Vandenbosch, M and Su Jung Kim (2013) Social media engagement that drives purchase behavior, in *Advances in Advertising Research (Vol. IV)*, Springer Fachmedien, Wiesbaden, pp 29–42

4 http://www.youtube.com/watch?v=IwE1zb9fiVs

5 http://www.huffingtonpost.com/2012/12/21/zappos-10-hour-call_n_2345467.html

6 'Net Promoter Score' was coined by Fred Reichheld in his book *The Ultimate Question* (Harvard Business School Press, 2006). The Net Promoter System™ is based on the fundamental perspective that every company's customers can be divided into three categories. 'Promoters' are loyal enthusiasts who keep buying from a company and urge their friends to do the same. 'Passives' are satisfied but unenthusiastic customers who can be easily wooed by the competition. 'Detractors' are unhappy customers trapped in a bad relationship. Customers can be categorized based on their answer to the ultimate question. The best way to gauge the efficiency of a company's growth engine is to take the percentage of customers who are promoters and subtract the percentage who are detractors. This equation is how we calculate a Net Promoter Score for a company.

7 Alexander, D L *et al* (2008) As time goes by: Do cold feet follow warm intentions for really new versus incrementally new products? *Journal of Marketing Research,* 45, June, 307–19

8 Meyer, R J *et al* (2008) Biases in valuation vs usage of innovative product features, *Marketing Science,* 27, 6, November–December, 1083–96

9 However, it has also been shown that the ideas coming from professionals are not necessarily more innovative and out-of-the-box than those coming from customers. Poetz, M K and Schreier, M (2012) The value of crowdsourcing: Can users really compete with professionals in generating new product ideas? *The Journal of Product Innovation Management,* 29, 2, 245–56

10 Anderson, K (2009) Ethnographic research: A key to strategy, *Harvard Business Review,* March

11 Leonard, D (1997) Spark innovation through empathic design, *Harvard Business Review,* November–December

12 http://www.vlerick.com/en/about-vlerick/Enjoy-Change/P-and-G/the-full-story

13 Dawar, N and Vandenbosch, M (2004) Seller's hidden advantage, *MIT Sloan Review*, winter

14 http://www.forbes.com/sites/meghancasserly/2012/02/16/pampers-or-huggies-how-diapers-com-profiles-customers-from-first-click/

15 http://www.theconversationmanager.com/2013/04/16/6-cases-where-marketing-and-technology-form-a-perfect-blend/?utm_source=rss&utm_medium=rss&utm_campaign=6-cases-where-marketing-and-technology-form-a-perfect-blend

16 Poetz, M and Schreier, M (2012) The value of crowdsourcing: Can users really compete with professionals in generating new product ideas? *Journal of Product Innovation Management,* 29, 2, 245–56

17 Boudreau, K J and Lakhani, K R (2009) How to manage outside innovation, *MIT Sloan Management Review,* Summer, 50, 4, 68–76

18 Gary Lilien and colleagues found that new product concepts jointly developed by carefully selected lead users collaborating with in-house personnel at 3M were characterized by higher innovativeness and showed a sales potential that was an average of eight times higher than traditionally developed 3M concepts. Lilien, G L *et al* (2002) Performance assessment of the lead user idea-generation process for new product development, *Management Science,* 48, 8, 1042–59

19 Prahalad, C K and Ramaswamy, V (2004) Co-creation experiences: the next practice in value creation, *Journal of Interactive Marketing,* 18, 3, 5–14

20 An online market research community can unite anywhere between 20 and 100 people in the discussion

21 InSites Consulting (2013) *The Consumer Consulting Board*, InSites Consulting, Ghent

22 This story was drawn from Shah, S K and Tripsas, M (2007) The accidental entrepreneur: The emergent and collective process of user entrepreneurship, *Strategic Entrepreneurship Journal,* 1, 1/2, 123–40

23 Von Hippel, E J *et al* (2012) Comparing business and household sector innovation in consumer products: Findings from a representative survey in the UK, *Management Science,* 58, 9, September, 1669–81

24 http://www.babyjogger.com/

25 Shah, S K (2003) Community-based innovation and product development: Findings from open source software and consumer sporting goods, Doctoral dissertation, MIT, Cambridge, MA

26 Cohen, P (2011) Innovation far removed from the lab, *New York Times,* 9 February

27 Shah, S K and Tripsas, M (2007) The accidental entrepreneur: The emergent and collective process of user entrepreneurship, *Strategic Entrepreneurship Journal,* 1, 1/2, 123–40

28 Von Hippel, E (2011) People don't need a profit motive to innovate, *Harvard Business Review,* November, 36–7

29 Von Hippel, E and Oliveira, P (2009) Users as service innovators: The case of banking services, *MIT Sloan School of Management Working Paper,* 4748-09

Convert the first lens by innovating every day

02

Be a moving target, not a sitting duck

> *If we don't constantly innovate, we do not deserve to survive.*
> **JACQUES HOROVITZ, CHÂTEAUFORM'**

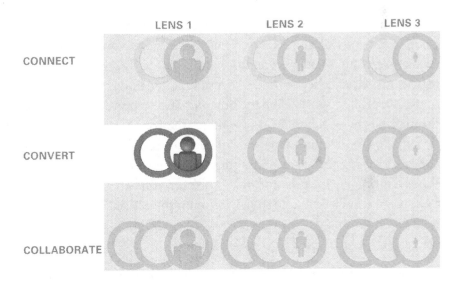

There has hardly been a more popular business topic in the last couple of years than innovation. Compelled by the idea that the only alternative to innovation is extinction, companies have made innovation one of their top strategic priorities. They have rolled out innovation programmes and appointed innovation leaders. Seduced by the shining example of aspirational leaders like Apple, the idea of being a game-changer has been more compelling than ever. Innovation recipes are discussed in blogs, opinion pieces, managers' journals and books. An Amazon search on the keyword 'innovation' yields well over 7,000 results. But in spite of all of this talk, companies still struggle with making innovation happen. One of the reasons is that the term 'innovation' seems have become confined to the big step-changes associated with radical breakthroughs. With that, it becomes an elusive, almost unattainable goal. The success of some radical innovations has undoubtedly created a fortune for some firms while leading to the demise of others. But the exclusive pursuit of radical innovation is detrimental. It means that the full innovation potential of the company is not exploited. And, as we will demonstrate, it even makes the organization less likely to generate or accept the elusive radical innovation that executives are looking for.

Incremental innovation and radical innovation are often depicted as opposite ends of a spectrum. They serve a different purpose and require separate practices. We think of the established business being in operational excellence mode, focused on keeping the train on the tracks. Radical innovation on the other hand is seen as creating breakthrough business, focused on rebuilding the train from scratch. But it is an illusion to think that we can be successful with radical innovation if we cannot successfully implement incremental innovation. When an organization is not able to incorporate the small innovation, it certainly is not able to deliver upon the radical breakthrough innovation. To make the organization more receptive to innovation, we have to make it used to constant change.

All the talk of innovation obscures the fact that innovation is not reserved only for the areas of disruptive change and radical breakthroughs. Innovation is just as much about the daily improvements and changes. While striving for the big step-changes, we forget the value that resides in making small steps every day. In the innovation spectrum, there should be room for radical as well as incremental innovation.

Incremental innovation refers to improvements to existing products and services to better suit the needs of current and potential customers.[1] Incremental innovations bring value to the business, and help you to be a moving target. Effective incremental product and service development and rapid consecutive introductions keep you ahead of the competition, established or new.[2] Research shows that introducing incremental innovations strongly influences a business's market share, performance and, indirectly, its survival in an established industry. Firms that are among the first to introduce important incremental innovations realize substantial market share advantages. But even if you are not the first, copycat innovation also contributes to market success. Keeping abreast of new developments creates less opportunities for competitors to use them as differentiators, and by doing so you assure longevity.

However, incremental innovation can also be a fatal trap. Unless it is inspired by customer needs, it can lead to a spiral of unwanted feature additions and meaningless differentiators. If companies only try to outrun competitors in an effort to distinguish their products from theirs, there is a danger of outrunning the customer at the same time. In essence, there are three dangers lurking around the corner with incremental innovation:

1 *Feature bloat.* This is where features are being piled on
   in an effort to differentiate from competition. Often the
   motivation is to meet all segments' needs and wishes with a
   single product (creating the 'Swiss army knife' of products:
   you can use it for everything!). The resulting feature creep
   eventually leads to feature fatigue with customers. Products
   are developed that are the answer to the question nobody
   asked![3] The digital camcorder leaders learnt this lesson the
   hard way when they were beaten by a start-up company
   that launched a cheap, small and simple camera that was in
   many ways inferior to the existing products.[4] But instead
   of having to read manuals the size of a Russian novel, users
   could use this camera right away. Two years after its launch,
   the Flip camera captured 20 per cent of the market, taking

incumbents with much more sophisticated products by total surprise.

2 *Overshooting.* Overshooting is where products and services start to exceed the requirements of the majority of the market. A signal of overshooting is when companies offer new attributes for which customers are increasingly unwilling to pay premium prices. Another signal is when the high-end segment of the market seems to become smaller and smaller. The type of customer who wants the best and is willing to pay for it becomes a rare specimen.

3 *Meaningless differentiation.* When all obvious options have been exhausted, the way to differentiate products and services is by searching for even the slightest difference that can distinguish you from competitors. This often leads to value presumption: when the seller's product or service possesses an attribute that is different from competitors, we automatically assume that customers will care about it, taking our own wishes for granted. Instead of offering differentiation that is really relevant for customers, we try to differentiate on trivial attributes that customers couldn't care less about.

Taking into account all of these issues, it is no wonder that incremental innovation has come to be associated with fruitless innovation efforts. The opposite is, however, true: incremental product innovation is a critically important competitive factor in established industries. We need to start cherishing innovation endeavours with a small i just as much as the capital I Innovation ones. But incremental innovation, perhaps even more than radical innovation efforts, needs to be entirely inspired by market requirements. It is based on a constant effort to translate what we learn from customers about what they want by way of improvements, modifications and innovations. The goal is to do this faster and more effectively than competitors, because it is totally attuned to the market. Outside-in organizations don't sit idle but constantly convert customer insights into changes in their offering.

Leverage a connected development model

Really listening to your customer is not a marketing gimmick. It's the fundamental driving force behind the company's strategy. This means that customers become active participants in their exchanges with the company, and get a say in the company's actions. The approach we propose contrasts the 'big bang' development model for new product development with a 'connected' development model; see Figure 2.1.

The 'big-bang' development model looks like this: new products are developed in secrecy, and new ideas are kept close to the chest. Customers are studied, after which we withdraw within our cocoon until we're ready to come back out with the product we expect they all have been waiting for. The goal is to deploy a streamlined process, based on a linear set of steps that minimize unnecessary iterations. The process unfolds based on the input and definition of a set of pre-defined, assumed customer requirements. While the big-bang development model may use customers during the process to test ideas on, customers are not further involved. Implicit in this view is a critical assumption that firms can act autonomously in designing products, developing production processes, crafting marketing messages, and

FIGURE 2.1 The connected development process

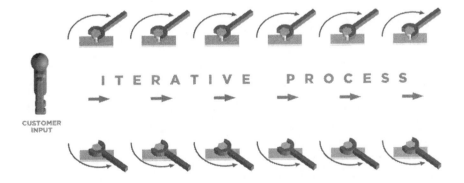

TABLE 2.1 Big bang versus connected development

	Big-bang development	Connected development
Customers' role	Reactive	Active
Degree of company control	High	Shared
Process	Closed, linear process	Open, iterative process
Key concern	Protecting confidentiality	Generating involvement
Guiding philosophy	Create for customers	Create with customers

controlling sales channels with little or no interference from or inter-action with consumers.[5] At the end of the process, the new product or service is finally revealed to the market, heavily supported by big communication budgets: the big bang!

Today, we are active in a world where the bar is being raised and we need more than the traditional linear approach. The 'connected' development model involves customers along the way, and they will be grateful for that involvement and increasingly demand it. In the 'connected' development model, we use an open and iterative process where customers are active participants. The differences between the approaches are set out in Table 2.1.

Close the feedback loop

To develop the benefits of a constant customer feedback loop, three steps need to be put in place. The first is to connect with customers and open the channels of communication, which we discussed in Chapter 1. The second step is to act on the input.

Closing the feedback loop is essential to gain any advantage from opening the gates of communication and to avoid any counter-productive effects. A customer communicating with you wants a

CASE STUDY

Take the example of Apple. Listening to customers isn't something Apple does once a year or even once a quarter. It plays a central role in the daily management of Apple's 300+ plus stores. Comments from customers help store managers prepare for service recovery calls with unhappy customers to close the feedback loop: store managers call every unhappy customer within 24 hours. The outcomes of these calls, together with the customer comments, provide important coaching and feedback messages that are passed along to employees.

Studies showed that unhappy customers who the store manager had talked to after their visit purchased substantially more Apple products and services than the others. Further studies showed that every hour spent calling unhappy customers was generating more than $1,000 in revenue or additional sales of $25 million in the first year. In other words, the effort put into calling customers is a worthwhile investment, and not an additional cost.[6]

reaction, and asking customers for their opinion without responding leads to a more negative evaluation than not asking for opinions at all. Acting on the input happens on two levels. The first is about an immediate response to individual customers.

The second level of acting on the input is when you analyse the feedback from customers at an aggregate level to uncover systemic patterns. The value from measuring customer satisfaction is not the metric itself; rather it is understanding what drives the score customers give you. What would it take for them to rate you higher? What is missing? What are the most obvious pain points that you need to solve for customers? Who are the customers that rate you higher? Do they represent a specific segment? Can you learn something from looking at the areas you score better at? What is it that you do differently there? Can you roll that out on a bigger scale? Spotting patterns enables you to correct systemic defects. On this level, customer comments and evaluations shape strategic choices and resource allocation.

Fixing the areas that lead to customer irritation in the end leads to lower costs. It allows you to remove the 20 per cent of things customer complain about 80 per cent of the time. Fixing things lowers the costs of complaint handling, product returns and reparations and customer service. Companies with satisfied customers have to spend less on service recovery, recovering lost customers and acquiring new customers to make up for the lost ones.[7]

Constant focus on micro-innovations

As outlined earlier, a successful outside-in strategy implementation starts with paying attention to everyday opportunities to improve products and services as a result of customer feedback and insights. To make this happen, innovation processes have to be embedded across the organization. Leaving the innovation initiatives only to those who have 'innovation' in their job description leads to a lot of unexploited potential opportunities. The responsibility for recognizing ways to add value for customers should be shared across the organization. It's a collective task, carried out by all – not just by those who are in the front line, dealing directly with customers.

Responding effectively to a market need usually requires the participation of different departments within an organization. This might include product management to conceptualize a new product, operations to make sure it can be manufactured, R&D to develop it, customer service to provide after-sales service, and so on. It's therefore paramount that information about customer insights is shared across departments and functions.[8] Having all involved and informed provides a shared basis for concerted action and prevents roadblocks along the way. If everybody clearly understands the customer motivation behind an initiative, it creates a common ground to make it happen. These principles are all illustrated in the range of practices that Châteauform' implements to foster continuous innovation.

CASE STUDY

The story of Châteauform' starts in 1996, when Professor Jacques Horovitz, a service marketing specialist, decided to create the unique concept of Chateauform Home of Seminars. Having taught in residential seminars for executive committees and business managers all over the world, he had noticed that appropriate areas for such seminars were hard to find. He saw the opportunity to build a completely new approach to residential seminars, starting from the customer's needs. From his observations, Horovitz had noticed that most seminar venues were often unsuitable and inadequate for the needs of corporate and professional groups. Meeting rooms were frequently uncomfortable or insufficiently equipped and recreational activities insufficient to enable participants to unwind, chat informally and get to know each other. Services lacked the flexibility to adapt to the needs of the groups and unforeseen participant requests were time-consuming and difficult for the assistants to satisfy. Any additional services requested were uniformly treated as extras, which often increased costs and decreased price transparency for the seminar planners. In short, the venues and the seminar operations detracted from the client group and seminar dynamics instead of enhancing them.

With this in mind, the Chateauform concept was born out of Horovitz's own country house in Neuville-Bosc, not far from Paris. It was to be the first of a series of venues specifically dedicated to corporate meetings, training events and workshops. Clients were immediately enthusiastic and soon thereafter new sites opened around Paris and later further across Europe. Today, Châteauform' is a company with more than €90 million in revenue, featuring double-digit growth since its inception.

Built on a culture of extreme customer focus, Châteauform' keeps a keen eye on improving what it offers to customers to make the overall service better tailored to their needs. This focus goes hand in hand with constantly questioning the current approach and offering. Nothing is sacred; everything can be challenged. Being a customer-focused organization requires continuous listening to customer demands and feedback. At Châteauform' that means processing 5 million 'Sweet or Sour' customer satisfaction surveys a year. It also means a culture of continuous adaptations in small and big changes to the offering to respond to customer concerns. The primary foundation for this is a core value of love for the customer. But continuous innovation is not just a matter of culture; it's also creating the processes to enable it to happen. With this goal in mind, Châteauform' implements a range of initiatives.

Sweet or Sour

During the last day of a seminar, each participant is asked to complete a satisfaction survey, called 'Sweet or Sour', on site. It asks for participants' names and enables them to rate their satisfaction regarding all aspects of their experience – from the service and organization (welcome, cleanliness, meals) to the site (general rooms, seminar rooms and leisure activities). In addition, participants are asked to indicate whether they would return and to what extent they would or would not recommend Châteauform' to others. As the 'Sweet or Sours' are completed on site, it is expected that the site management will use them right away to fix issues participants had alerted them to.

The response rate for the 'Sweet and Sour' form is over 90 per cent. All the feedback received is systematically analysed by the customer relations team and compiled into monthly reports. The comments are aggregated and form the starting point for investment made each year at the locations. The qualitative feedback from customers forms a continuous source of inspiration to make improvements and to delight customers and exceed their expectations.

Customer advisory board

The customer advisory board brings a set of customers together every year for a weekend at Châteauform'. They are invited to spend time in an informal way with the management and engage in feedback sessions on the issues and unresolved problems they have as well as to brainstorm about new ideas they would like Châteauform' to implement.

Golden eye

Châteauform' does not only ask the customer for feedback but also asks its employees. The main idea is that an external perspective is a 'Golden eye'. Every Châteauform' location has a notebook available, called the 'Golden book', the aim of which is to capture concrete ideas and suggestions employees have for each other and for the organization.

Employees are encouraged to notice points of improvement and to write them down in the 'Golden book'. The book makes for a neutral, not person-specific, way to give feedback. Having the book takes away the need to put people on the spot with their ideas and suggestions.

Week 'in another way'

Every year, the executive management spends a week doing one of the employees' jobs. Not only does it give them a renewed appreciation for the tasks carried out by the people whose role they take over, it is also a confrontation with the day-to-day operational processes. As such, it is always a source of new ideas on how to improve things.

Laboratory of new ideas

The laboratory of new ideas represents a group of people who have the formal mandate to come up with new ideas and to test them out. They meet regularly to share ideas and discuss how to move them forward.

Annual fair of new ideas

Every year an open fair is organized where people can present the new things they have implemented at their location. Any site that has an idea can try it and, if it works, they present it at the annual open fair. Through this, best practices are shared, and others can adopt them.

What is clear is that the continuous focus on customer-oriented improvements and innovations does not depend on a single management process. It is not just one practice. It's a series of initiatives that exploit all opportunities to foster incremental innovation. At the same time, this range of concerted initiatives creates a broad basis that installs a culture of continuous change and innovation within the organization. What is also apparent from the story of Châteauform' is that innovation is not driven by the motivation to outperform competitors. It is completely driven by the desire to fulfil customer needs better.

Make it organization-wide

One of the biggest mistakes is to assume that direct customer feedback is only relevant for the frontline departments. Companies that are serious about integrating a constant customer feedback loop into their processes do not delegate the job to the sales and marketing department, service department or to local branches. Senior leadership gets directly involved. Departments that do not directly interact with customers are kept fully in the loop.[9]

First, senior leadership teams that communicate directly with and about customers send an important signal both inside and outside the company. They show that they care, and that the customer is a key priority. They demonstrate that customer-centricity plays a bigger role than being part of a glorified mission statement that gathers dust in a strategy report. It is crucial to document customer insights in a way that is easy for employees to understand and share. This can happen through workshops, stories, pamphlets. All these help narrate the customer input.

Second, sharing across the organization enables non-customer-facing departments to better understand their role in meeting customer requirements and create the conditions that help the organization to focus better on customer needs. Staff and support departments often create boundaries that may facilitate or hinder customer-facing departments in doing a good job. An example is the IT department of a large retail bank: as it specifies the CRM system's functionality, it directly affects how sales people will be able to relate to customers on an individual level.

Finally, sharing information about customers and how they evaluate the products and services from the company creates a culture where the customer is seen as important. What you focus attention on is a key indicator of what you value. Companies where customers are never a topic of conversation or never on the agenda clearly do not consider customers an important enough issue to talk about. But what about the company where every department's meeting always starts with reviewing the latest customer comments? Clearly, everybody

Mirror, mirror on the wall

There is no substitute for direct customer feedback, as the people manning the customer service lines at your company will testify. But why reserve the experience of getting direct customer feedback only for the people in the frontlines?

Make it company policy to have everybody share in this direct feedback from customers.

will understand that customers are everybody's business and that, in the end, it is the customer who pays every employee's wages.

Harness the full potential

As the story of Châteauform' illustrates, making improvements to products and services and creating continuous incremental innovation is not the sole responsibility of one person or department. It does not depend on a visionary leader; rather it is the result of a company-wide, shared responsibility. If we can mobilize this responsibility, we can harness the full potential of the organization. Often lots of ideas can lay hidden within the organization; we just need to pull them out. For that, we need to encourage and facilitate, and provide a catalyst for growing the ideas from within.[10]

Internal innovation communities can foster this process. They provide a platform for employees to share and discuss ideas. Companies like Eli Lilly and Deloitte have set up (online) innovation communities to create an easily accessible place for innovation enthusiasts to come together. To ignite involvement, they complement the online tools with offline gatherings.

An internal community like this can have a big impact on the company culture. The first step to increasing innovativeness is to foster inspiration within the organization, which is reflected in the corporate culture. The purpose is to change the mindset of the people by

CASE STUDY

Such an initiative was also developed at a large consumer electronics company. The project started with setting up creativity rooms – areas for employees to have creative thoughts. Within these areas, brainstorming sessions are organized. Outsiders, so called 'wild geese' may be invited, to provide fresh perspectives. The company also organizes lectures and provides a library with inspiring literature within the creativity room. The inspiration sessions are organized around various topics, not necessarily related to the company's products or markets.

The online idea forum was afterwards created to provide a way to follow-up on the ideas created during the inspiration sessions. The forum is mainly internally used although sometimes external experts in various domains are invited to join the community. The community was created to foster innovative ideas and to contribute to the change of corporate culture into a more entrepreneurial one – and it succeeded in doing so: in three years about 500 ideas have been gathered. Often people enter the discussion who do not have a direct stake in the project within their day-to-day job, but nevertheless have useful input. One of the products, which came out of this community forum was a TV stand and wall mounting combined in one item. This idea came from a person working as a cost accountant and is a perfect example of how diversity brings more creativity into a community.

There are also physical ideation sessions organized, to which selected external people are invited to get the most out of the creative potential of the employees. These run for a day and a half. (Due to the high interest within the broader organization, physical sessions have been virtualized and there is a series of 'happy hours' during the day on a virtual platform.) A further off-line event is an innovation fair, where all successful new ideas are introduced as prototypes to the marketing department and C-level management.

empowering them. By creating a community with the explicit goal of harnessing innovation ideas from within, awareness is created about the role that all employees can play in the process. It brings to the surface that everybody has the opportunity to contribute, and also gets the formal mandate to do so.

Across a company with many divisions and areas, innovation communities can act like a silo breaker and enable the company to get a multidisciplinary view on ideas. An organization-wide innovation portal endorses collaboration. It is also through the confrontation of different perspectives that new ideas emerge that would have originated from a single functional perspective. In order to be innovative we need people from one division to see the ideas of people from another, and to comment on them so they can be developed further, and that is the idea behind this network.

In short

- End the exclusive love affair with breakthrough innovation projects: savour small innovation just as much as big innovation.
- Let customer needs be the inspiration and starting point for all innovation initiatives.
- Close the feedback loop on two different levels. First, take immediate action in the case of customers who are not fully satisfied. Second, uncover systemic patterns and translate them into process improvements and new products and services.
- Never stand still. Keep a constant focus on micro-innovations.
- Sharing customer feedback across the organization is important. Dealing with customers is not just the role of frontline and commercial people. Everybody within the organization in some way creates the conditions that enable the company to respond effectively to customer needs.
- By sharing customer information internally, a culture of customer-centricity is fostered.

Get started

- Set up a process to close the feedback loop with customers.
- Regularly review customer feedback, and set up an action plan to tackle issues and ideas.

- Stop dismissing micro-innovation as 'not being innovative'.

- Set up a range of initiatives to involve employees in your constant innovation efforts.

Notes

1 Varadarajan, R (2009) Fortune at the bottom of the innovation pyramid. The strategic logic of incremental innovations, *Business Horizons,* 52, 21–29

2 Banbury, C and Mitchell, W (1995) The effect of introducing important incremental innovation on business performance and survival, *Strategic Management Journal,* 16, 161–81

3 Rust, R *et al* (2006) Defeating feature fatigue, *Harvard Business Review,* February

4 Stone, B (2008) Start-up releases smaller version of flip camcorder, *New York Times,* June

5 Prahalad, C K and Ramaswamy, V (2004) Co-creation experiences: the next practise in value creation, *Journal of Interactive Marketing,* 18, 3, 5–14

6 Reichheld, F (2011) The ultimate question 2.0, *Harvard Business Review Press,* Cambridge, MA

7 Reichheld, F (2011) The ultimate question 2.0, *Harvard Business Review Press,* Cambridge, MA

8 Kohli, A K and Jaworski, B J (1990) Market orientation: The construct, research propositions, and managerial implications, *Journal of Marketing,* 54, 2, 1–18

9 Kohli, A K and Jaworski, B J (1990) Market orientation: The construct, research propositions, and managerial implications, *Journal of Marketing,* 54, 2, 1–18

10 Martin, R (2011) Innovation in the front lines, *Harvard Business Review,* June

Collaborate with customers

03

Put customers at the core

> *When given the choice of obsessing over competitors or obsessing over customers, we always obsess over customers.*
> **JEFF BEZOS**

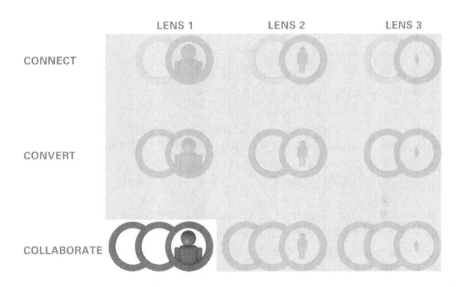

Exploiting the first lens means that you put your customer at the heart of everything you do.

CASE STUDY

Take the example of car-sharing service Zipcar, the global leader in its field. Zipcar is often cited as the first true example of collaborative consumption. On 14 March 2013 Avis Budget Group purchased Zipcar for about US $500 million in cash. When it was founded in 2000, Zipcar was one of the pioneers of the 'sharing economy', where physical goods are shared among a group of people, rather than individually owned. The company came from nowhere into a rental car business dominated by giants such as Hertz and Avis, creating a new market of by-the-hour rentals. Meanwhile, the car rental incumbents focused on battling each other at long-standing airport locations. While the giants continue to duke it out, Zipcar has captured 80 per cent of the industry it created, largely unbothered by any of the existing players in the car rental industry.

The key to the company's success according to co-founder Robin Chase was: 'The customers were front and centre in building the business.' When Chase started Zipcar in Cambridge, Massachusetts in 2000 with Antje Danielson, the duo re-envisioned the way people use cars in urban areas. Instead of lengthy waits at rental car counters, Zipcar pioneered the use of technology that allowed customers to reserve cars online, using membership cards to unlock vehicles at specific locations. It quickly found a niche with a mostly young, hip customer base who instantly grasped how grabbing a car for an hour or two from a nearby spot could fit into their busy lives. Zipcar has since gone from being an interesting idea to the leader in car sharing, with about 770,000 members at year-end 2012, $280 million in revenue, $17.2 million EBITDA and a year-to-year revenue growth rate of 17 per cent.

Car rental is a commodity business with rather low margins; what is Zipcar doing that inspires loyalty far beyond the traditional players in the space? First of all, Zipcar does not see itself as being in the car rental business, but rather in the shared car ownership service business. The company has a keen view on exactly who its core customers are. It's a young (20 or early 30-something), carless, childless, relatively affluent, and likely single person living in a dense area of a big city. In other words, people who see themselves as making lifestyle choices contrary to the dominant ones in the United States. In a country where car ownership (outside of select metro areas) is nearly universal, not having a car is a strong statement of values – environmental and financial values chief among them – and Zipcar doesn't just recognize this in its marketing materials, it plays an active role in helping consumers with these values achieve their goals. The company understands that for its customers, access is more important than ownership. Everything about the company – from its marketing to its customer interface to its rules – supports that identity. As a result, Zipcar customers see the company as part of their way of life, rather than a mere service provider. Since its inception, Zipcar has continuously adapted its value proposition to better suit the needs of its core customers. Except for the occasional pickup and luxury car, the entire fleet is fuel-efficient and much of it is Toyota Priuses. They're located in the neighbourhoods where Zipcar's consumers live, in easy-to-reach places.

Zipcar's customers, known as Zipsters, are fiercely loyal to the brand. Zipcar makes continuous efforts to rope consumers into the brand, through comprehensive wrapping of vehicles in Zipcar branding to 'Zipster' events and discounts at area retailers and restaurants. A popular activity among Zipcar's Facebook fans is sharing pictures from road trips they've taken in their rented cars. Creating a sense of community of mutual respect and respect for others is a critical aspect of the business. Zipcar has spent a lot of time fine-tuning the parameters that foster its community, such as how it encourages people to keep cars clean and how fees are imposed for returning a car late. The company encourages its members to have a spirit of bonding together to make the world a better place.[1]

The conventional rental car experience is worlds away. You feel no communal connection to your fellow renters, and you are renting because you have no choice. Avis and its rental competitors are largely interchangeable commodities for most customers. Zipcar on the other hand has built a hard-to-replicate asset by fostering a customer community based on shared values. Despite the complexity of Zipcar's operations (in multiple cities and countries, across varying channels and touch-points, in a relatively new business category), it maintains a unified strategic core focus on experience. In whatever it does, the focus is always on how its choices impact the members' experience. Understanding members' experiences starts from fieldwork; even the COO has done some 'ride-along' trips with members. This is driven by the belief that if you're not observing people and making an earnest attempt to understand what they are experiencing while using your product/service, it is impossible to design a product/service with a focus on their experience. Focus groups, surveys and quantitative data may be useful, but there's no substitute for real in-market, in-field observation and discussion with end-users.[2]

The Zipcar story shows how companies have a lot to gain from keeping the customer close and by fostering customer communities. By doing so, the company not only fosters a bond between the customers and the company but also amongst the customers themselves.

Walk in through the same door

- Enter your retail location through the front door, in fact search for a parking spot first. Go to your website and experience every click customers have to make to find the information they're looking for, without the shortcuts and passwords that are available to you.

- The aim of the 'walk in through the same door' exercise is to go through the customer experience you provide in exactly the same way as your customers would.

- It is an exercise to follow the same path as your customer would: when looking for info on your website, when looking for a product, when navigating through your store.

That building strong customer connections is a foundation for competitive advantage is recognized by many of today's business leaders. Customer intimacy is foremost on CEOs' minds: 88 per cent of all CEOs nominate getting closer to the customer as the most important dimension to realize their strategy in the next five years. These CEOs are convinced they must not only stay connected (or reconnect) with customers, but keep on learning how to strengthen those bonds.[3]

Success comes from successfully mobilizing two parties: customers and employees. The essential party to collaborate with to become an outside-in organization is the customer. Our mission is to build deep engagement with customers, based on structural collaboration rather than a distant relationship. We literally need to bring customers 'inside' the business. This means changing the paradigm from discussing value for the customer and the value of the customer to creating value *with* the customer. Instead of keeping customers outside of the organization, we involve them as much as possible. Customers are involved all the way. Instead of testing products on customers, we design them with customers. Instead of sending communication messages to customers, we talk to customers and encourage them to talk to each other. Co-creation is the new paradigm.

The reverse value chain on which the outside-in organization is based starts from the customer. But this customer is not an entity outside of the company: it's an integrated part of the company. As a result of this, the depth of the connections that we build with customers is the source of competitive advantage. The switching costs created are hard for any competitor to overcome, the deep connection and bond difficult to replace. But companies clearly still struggle to make customer-centricity more than an intention. In the following sections we describe the key behaviours that characterize companies that are able to cultivate structural collaborations with customers.

Create a platform to bring customers together

Online communities have become an essential part of fostering customer engagement. These communities usually serve as a market telescope for a company allowing it to get closer to its customers. They facilitate the conversation and allow the company to tap into its customer base on a continuous basis. And while they create the channel for a dialogue between a company and its customers, they also create lateral communication between customers. Creating customer communities is a way to not only have customers talk to you but also to each other. Bringing customers together can completely alter the role that a company plays in relation to them, and open up new avenues for growth. A clear story that illustrates this point is SWIFT and its Innotribe initiative.

CASE STUDY

SWIFT sets the standards for international financial transactions, and runs a highly secure and reliable network (or intranet) connecting 8,000 banks and 1,500 major corporations across the globe. SWIFT has a strong company culture of 'Failure Is Not An Option' (FNAO), which is essential given that even a couple of seconds of downtime could have a major impact on financial transactions across the globe. Although this culture was inspired by the Apollo 13 mission, where the NASA team would do 'whatever it takes' to get the three astronauts back from space, over the years the FNAO mantra was at times misinterpreted as a culture of no risk taking, not coming up with ideas challenging the status quo, not daring to step forward.[4] To combat this culture, Innotribe started in 2009 as an internal company tool aimed at two main functions: changing the company culture to a more innovative one and changing the company positioning to the outside world. As SWIFT exists by virtue of the community of banking institutions it supports, the mission was to enable collaborative innovation amongst that community. SWIFT is in the unique position of a central node that enables it to create an innovation hub for banks around the world.

Innotribe started by bringing together bright minds from within and outside the company and giving them an opportunity to realize their business ideas. The effort started internally with the idea of 'megaphones' – internal innovation ambassadors in different departments of the company. In the initial version, megaphones were 'volunteered', their mandate was unclear and their management was not motivated or incentivized. Later on megaphones were recruited through an internal campaign, and received a clear mandate: spend 15 per cent of their time on innovation-related activities, as part of their objectives, and signed-off at the beginning of the year by their managers.

The Innotribe initiative continued with setting up a platform for individuals to come together and discuss innovation initiatives in the financial world. The 'Start-Up Challenge' is probably one of the most visible initiatives: in 2012 more than 600 start-up companies were screened during three regional competitions (one for the Americas, one for EMEA and one for APAC), and the two winners received a $50,000 cash prize. The basic objective of this initiative is to bridge the gap between the start-up community and the heads of innovation of the financial industry. One success story illustrates this: MasterCard acquired the winner of the 2011 edition in 2012 for $40 million.

A new channel of meaningful communication within the company was created, and opened up the company to the outside world. Kosta Peric, innovation leader at SWIFT says: 'Our customers love it. We see tribe behaviour – like fans for life, groupies – and return customers, who come back only for the Innotribe vibe and connections. Customers declare it is "their" Innotribe.' The Innotribe brand has now become synonymous with collaborative innovation in the financial services community; the Innotribe brand had a strong positive effect on the overall SWIFT brand. Lazzaro Campo, SWIFT CEO referred to the Innotribe brand as the 'strongest brand SWIFT has produced in the last 30 years'.[5]

This example shows that fostering customer communities is not reserved for the online environment, nor is it only valid for B2C companies. Specifically for B2B companies, the use of customer communities provides the opportunity to create a different type of conversation with your customers. A conversation where the talk is not about the next order, or the last quality gaffe, but one that is future-oriented. The nature of the discussion is less about 'how much more can we sell to you' and more about 'what are the issues that we will face tomorrow'. It creates a dialogue that broadens the topics explored to the issues that customers face in their business. As a result, the company initiating the customer community is showing itself as a potential partner to talk to about new solutions. It's also showing itself as a partner to get customers to talk to each other. By putting yourself in a position of being the central facilitator in a discussion about customers' business, you show yourself as interested in their issues, not yours. Inspiring and feeding an industry dialogue demonstrates that you are an expert in the customer's business. But a successful customer community, whether online or offline, requires a goal of structural collaboration. It's not a one-off initiative but a long-term approach.

Harvest all customer roles

Using the first lens, we connect with our existing customer base and market by building deep connections that foster a structural collaboration between the company and its customers. To do this, we need to look beyond customers as mere buyers of our products and services, and give them a much more active role. It is by expanding customers' roles that we create a deeper engagement with them. Sergio Zyman, former CMO at Coca-Cola, famously said: 'The sole purpose of marketing is to sell more stuff more often to more people for more money.' Ironically, it is by solely focusing on this goal of selling more to more people that we get further removed from it. The reason is that it puts customers only in the role of buyer. Today we realize that we need to take the focus off the push-approach of inducing customers to buy more stuff, and start understanding how we need to create value together with customers.

By narrow-mindedly seeing customers only in their role as buyers, we short-change both them and ourselves. It is by giving customers a more active position that we can leverage the customer base. Conventionally, customers are passive recipients of market strategies. The only vote they have is with their wallet. They voice themselves through their purchase (or lack thereof). Creating close connections with customers means involving them. There are many ways customers can create value for your company: they can be consultants, advisers, guides, co-creators and developers. To unleash the value of these other roles that customers can perform, we need to provide the platform to enable them to do so. Creating value with the customer can only happen if we are willing to see customers taking up these roles, and not see them as a threat – expanding on these roles gives companies a more solid foundation to grow their customer base.[6]

Customers as advocates

Word-of-mouth is the most effective marketing communication channel. This has long been recognized as a fundamental truth. But few companies have understood how they can tap into the potential that positive customer-to-customer communication can generate. For that, we need to make sure that customers take the advocacy role. The Olympic minimum for that to happen is that customers are satisfied; exceeding their expectation is often necessary to get any significant word-of-mouth effect. When you succeed in doing so, it can be a formidable engine of growth. Châteauform', introduced in Chapter 2, grew for 12 years purely by word-of-mouth. It could not keep up with customer demand, built without having to invest a single penny in marketing communication.

Aside from investing in delivering positive experiences for customers that leave them so happy that they spontaneously spread the word, what can a company do to ignite customer ambassadorship? Frontrunner companies do not leave it to chance, but actively set up ambassadorship programmes.

CASE STUDY

Take the example set by Salesforce.com. Using customers as advocates has been central to the Salesforce.com strategy from the start. Salesforce.com was founded by Marc Benioff, a former Oracle executive, in 1999. The initial premise was to make CRM applications accessible to small and medium-sized companies. Since then the company has grown to $3 billion in revenue from a multitude of cloud applications focusing on sales, marketing and communication.

The Salesforce.com market approach highlights the company's 'rock star' customers, using their stories and testimonials to inform prospects and guide them through the buying process. By putting the spotlight on other users, Salesforce.com relies on its customers to tell their story and convince prospective customers. Its yearly Dreamforce event is the ultimate fancy fair of Salesforce.com advocates, bringing together more than 40,000 users, prospects, enthusiasts and industry observers.

Unlike other CRM vendors that focus on IT professionals and high-level decision makers, Salesforce.com focuses on the user. The company publicly recognizes the user 'heroes' who create positive business results for their company using the platform provided by Salesforce. The ultimate status is reserved for their 80-something customer-users who get the privileged invitation to be part of the Salesforce.com MVP community. MVPs are selected because they are frontrunners in their community, excellent brand ambassadors and willing to engage in discussions with Salesforce about new developments. According to Salesforce.com the key characteristics of an outstanding MVP candidate include:[7]

- *Accessibility* – participating in the community at least nine days per month, either on success.salesforce.com or through social channels (blogs, Twitter, Facebook and LinkedIn).

- *Expertise* – having a strong understanding of the product and the needs of the community.

- *Responsive* – responding regularly to questions and contributing to the knowledge of the community.

- *Leadership* – representing the spirit of the community and bringing the voice of the customer back to salesforce.com.

- *Advocacy* – being a brand advocate for the product and jumping in to defend the company when necessary.

MVPs receive unique perks but are also clearly told that responsibilities come with the role.[8] They are Salesforce's biggest brand ambassadors. The benefits that they receive in return are all non-monetary, but they elevate the status of the person within and outside of their own organization. Salesforce.com puts the spotlight on its MVPs during events and in its own communication. As a return they are also invited to speak at Dreamforce, and have the selective opportunity of getting privileged insights from Salesforce.com product and marketing teams and are invited to mingle with high-level executives and CEO Marc Benioff. They get the front row seats at Dreamforce, where they might see The Red Hot Chili Peppers perform on stage. MVPs typically mention their status on their resume, and highlight their Salesforce MVP status on social media.

Customers as guides

As one Salesforce MVP member confessed in a blog post: 'One thing that I've learned about my fellow Salesforce MVPs is that they like talking about Salesforce just as much as I do.' This means MVPs help other customers with expert knowledge and insight. Part of being an MVP involves writing blogs that teach others tips, tricks or just give useful Salesforce info. Active members also answer questions on LinkedIn, in the Dreamforce app, using #askforce on Twitter, or on the Answers boards. They also organize user groups and promote learning about Salesforce. They share tips and tricks on how to get most out of the functionality and become a more sophisticated user. In other words: they do all sorts of things that normally would be the exclusive terrain of the customer service department of Salesforce.com.

Increasingly, companies realize that customers can be excellent guides to other customers. They start to mix brand and customer experts to provide or extend their own customer service model. Customers can give peer-to-peer customer support, help others with problems or advise them in choosing the right product. The idea of using customers as guides is based on the principle that customers are often well-positioned to do so. Through their own experiences, they often have relevant information to share with others who face similar issues.

Customers who are enthusiastic will often naturally take up the role of advisers to others and will cherish opportunities to share their knowledge. Amazon recognized this early on as it allowed reviews from readers on its website. The information you read there may be raw, subjective and biased, and deviates from the polished text that publishers provide, but it is relevant for other readers and increases the value of the Amazon site.

Customers as advisers

More and more companies are assembling a customer advisory board. This usually is a small group that gets together offline as well as online to discuss and advise on the company's strategy for the future. With this companies can engage people who are their ambassadors and who want to have a voice. Unlike an online idea board, a customer advisory board is not intended to get immediate new product ideas from customers. Rather it is to have an open discussion about the strategic issues facing the company and the industry at large.

Membership is typically made up of 10–30 senior executives. Obviously they represent some of the most important customers, but there needs to be variety and different points of view present. Topics of discussion tend to be more strategic than tactical. A customer advisory board is an opportunity to talk about broader issues than the tactical day-to-day ones. It allows you to keep in touch with what is going on in the customers' business and what their pressing issues are. (That means that you should not only discuss your own industry; much more relevant is discussing the customer's industry!) Customer advisory board members participate on a voluntary basis for the opportunity to influence company direction, in a way that is beneficial to their own needs, as well as the wider customer base. There is an expectation that the organization will follow through on key recommendations made. A customer advisory board in that respect almost functions like a shadow strategy board.

Customers as idea screeners

In earlier chapters we discussed a number of examples of large scale initiatives to gather new product ideas from customers, such as the Adidas Insiders and the Eurex board. Starbucks is another example.

CASE STUDY

One of the pioneers in creating a customer community is Starbucks, which set up an online community to foster communication with customers and to capture the ideas that customers had about what Starbucks should do to improve its product offering and experience. On MyStarbucks.com everyone is invited to co-shape the future of Starbucks by submitting their ideas, discussing them with others and voting on their favourite ideas. In the five years of My Starbucks' existence, Starbucks has turned 275 consumer-generated ideas into reality. Customers submitted more than 150,000 ideas, and 2 million votes were cast. Customers today can order a 'skinny' beverage and a cake pop, garner digital rewards for using their Starbucks Card and enjoy free Wi-Fi – all thanks to suggestions from fans.

The rewards for Starbucks? A continuous channel to monitor customer sentiment; a community that weeds out the ideas that they consider to be most valuable; a barometer to gauge customer interest in new ideas; but mostly, a customer community that feels part of Starbucks.

A few companies are brave enough to hand over control of idea selection to the community. That's what Lego did within its Lego Cuusoo community:

In our pilot community now, we employed the 'wait and see' approach and we do not select ideas we want to integrate. This is mainly because we do not want new product ideas, we want business partners with new ideas about our products. We promised that for 1,000 votes we will create a concept from an idea. You should see what kind of traffic this approach generates – the members are so busy promoting their ideas and pulling new people into the community, it is amazing… This year we will have our first product originating from the community in the market.[9]

Similarly, Amazon is giving control of the selection of TV shows to produce to its customers. As announced in the Q1 2013 statement: 'Amazon Studios is working on a new way to green-light TV shows. The pilots are out in the open where everyone can have a say.' According to Jeff Bezos, founder and CEO of Amazon.com:

I have my personal picks and so do members of the Amazon Studios team, but the exciting thing about our approach is that our opinions don't matter. Our customers will determine what goes into full-season production. We hope Amazon Originals can become yet another way for us to create value for Prime members.

The point is clear: using customers to generate ideas is an excellent way to foster a structural collaboration between a company and its customers.

Customers as designers

When you order a coffee at Starbucks, the choices you can make are virtually endless: tall or grande? Skinny or regular? Extra foam? Vanilla, pumpkin or plain? The result is a coffee that is your personal blend of choices. Products and processes should no longer be designed to standard specs, but be designed so that customers can still customize to fit their needs. Is that because customers really want a unique product? Because it's impossible to satisfy all and predict exactly what customers desire? Yes, to some extent. But it is also because the involvement in the design process leads to a greater engagement with the product. When we give customers the role of designers, we go further than just incorporating their ideas. In fact, we enable each customer to design the product just for them.

CASE STUDY

At Disney, you can design your own roller coaster ride using a touch screen on a computer. The Sum of All Thrills, at Epcot Theme Park, is a simulated thrill ride that counts on your creativity and brain power. You innovate and then experience the creation in a state-of-the-art robotic simulator.

How it works is simple. Visitors to the exhibit use a touch screen to design a roller coaster, bobsled, or jet ride, while adding features like hill climbs, dive rolls and corkscrews. After designing, the information is saved on a special card. The card is then swiped at a 'launch station' and your creative work is instantly uploaded to the simulator. Next, you enter the simulator's seating chamber where a 3-D video hood is placed over your head and upper torso. Now, the fun begins – twists and turns come alive in first-person point of view.[10]

Aside from being a great example of customer involvement in tailoring the product, The Sum of All Thrills is also a great example of collaboration between two partners. Walt Disney Imagineering worked with Raytheon to create and design The Sum of All Thrills. Raytheon, a military contractor, sponsored the attraction as part of its corporate philanthropy programme to interest young people in maths, science, technology and engineering.

Customers as employees

CASE STUDY

Take the story of Threadless, which built revenue of more than $30 million, selling an age-old product like T-shirts.

Its hip, cutting-edge T-shirts that speak to Generation Y consumers are not the result of the labour of Threadless designers. Instead, the company turns the fashion business on its head by enabling anyone to submit designs and asking its community of more than 500,000 members to help in selecting winning designs. Threadless churns out dozens of new items a month, with no advertising, no professional designers, no sales force and no retail distribution. The company ships as many as 10,000 orders a day from its Near West Side headquarters, where 65 full-time employees and another 30 part-timers work in a loft among ping-pong tables and an Airstream aluminium trailer.

How does it work? Threadless runs design competitions on its online social network. Members submit their ideas for T-shirts and then vote on which ones they like best. People use the site as a kind of community centre, where they blog, chat about designs, socialize with their fellow enthusiasts and of course also buy T-shirts. Revenue has been growing in double digits each year, despite the fact that the company has never advertised, employed no professional designers, used no modelling agency or fashion photographers, has no formal sales force, and has only one retail store.[11] You can buy a T-shirt on Threadless without participating in the design and voting process but research shows that only 5 per cent are buying without first voting on designs. Threadless customers are not simply consuming: they are actively participating in the company's core process.

The story of Threadless illustrates how far a company can go in giving customers an active role, taking up tasks that normally would be done by employees and kept inside the company's boundaries. It's clear that these boundaries are shifting and that customers increasingly become part of the company. You don't necessarily have to go as far as Threadless. Simply making customers a part of their own experience and giving them ownership already improves their satisfaction.

CASE STUDY

Think about the following scenario. You arrive at the airport for a long-planned intercontinental flight, only to find that it has been cancelled due to weather conditions at your destination. The agent at the airline counter you approach acknowledges the inconvenience but assures you that you can be rebooked on another flight. The agent asks you to wait in the lounge while he rebooks you. After 10 minutes, the agent calls you and explains that he was able to book you on a new flight that departs in three hours. You are relieved to hear that you will arrive at your destination anyway, albeit later than expected, and gratefully accept the rebooking. Case closed, and everybody happy in the end. Even with the mishap, the service recovery of the airline seemed to have gone smoothly: the necessary processes were in place and the responsible agent handles the situation well. But the scenario could have gone even better. Instead of sending you to the lounge, the agent could have asked you to stand with him to look for alternatives. Both of you could have been involved in searching the alternatives available, looking at the computer screen together. You could have been in a direct dialogue with the agent, asking questions, and telling him which of the alternatives you would prefer.

Assuming the outcome was exactly the same, which of the two scenarios would leave you the most satisfied and the most likely to fly again with this airline?

As it turns out, the second scenario, in which you as a customer play an active role instead of a passive one, leaves you with a more positive attitude about the airline, and more likely to fly again with them.[12]

The lesson learnt: we don't necessarily have to solve problems for customers, but rather solve problems *with* the customer. If it's efficient, easy and fast, customers even prefer to solve their own problems. Research shows that 40 per cent of consumers globally would prefer a self-service application than human contact.[13] Whereas we used to think about self-service technologies and processes as efficiency tools for companies, it's become apparent that customers also like them. Customers who are enabled to play an active part feel like they have a voice in tailoring to their needs. They feel more in control of the situation, and this in turn leaves them feeling better and satisfied with the outcome.

The key conclusion is that it is important to actively involve customers, and to empower them to take ownership of tasks that normally would fit firmly within the company's boundaries. Treating customers as employees means that we should involve them in processes and activities that typically would be taken up by our own people. Sharing responsibility and ownership of these processes with customers allows them to tailor better to their needs, to be actively engaged with the company and, in the end, to feel more like they are part of the company rather than an outsider. Inevitably, this leads to a stronger relationship.

In this section, we have explained how the role of customers can transcend beyond the role as buyer. Customers can be advocates, advisers, guides, idea generators, designers and employees. The message is clear: make customers part of your team. Involve customers, not by asking them what they want but by making them an integral part of your value chain. By opening ourselves up for customers we create a structural collaboration with our most important stakeholder. The benefits are a stronger bond with customers, and a win-win for both customers and the company. In the end customers are engaged with you, rather than just buying from you, and engaged customers create a plethora of benefits:

- They are more likely to buy, more often, and for more money.
- They refer other potential customers to you.
- They defend you when confronted with negative comments from other customers.
- They are willing to speak on your behalf, and have more credibility to do so.
- They provide more credible testimonials than anything you could say.
- They keep you grounded, as the trust relationship opens up the channel of conversation.

What all this is telling us is this: the driving force of customer innovation is not 'build it for them and they will come' but rather 'build it with them, and they're already there'.[14]

Go inside-out to enable outside-in

While the focus is on creating customer engagement, it would be an illusion to think that we can build a successful strategic collaboration with customers if we cannot do it first with our own employees.

Getting close to customers is not so much a problem the IT or marketing department needs to solve as a journey the whole organization needs to make. There's a chain of effects that lead to results from customer collaboration efforts. This chain starts on the inside.

Happy customers start with happy employees.[15] Investing in customers thus starts with investing in employees. Not only do we depend on employees to share a common purpose and to go the extra mile to create satisfied customers, employees are also the first breeding ground for customer advocacy. After all, if your own people are not your advocates, how can you expect other people to be?

CASE STUDY

I once delivered a workshop with the management team of a large multinational company in the residential services business.[16] The purpose of the workshop was to start developing a customer acquisition strategy for an existing service the company wanted to grow in revenue. The management team were adamant there was a great potential in the market, and touted the many benefits of the service. Sales projections in their business plan were highly optimistic. They described the target group as very similar to themselves: middle-class, dual earners, frequent travellers, with a family... and they reassured me that there were many reasons why this target group would need and want the service. But when I asked the people in the room who used the service themselves, it became remarkably silent... none of them did.

The making of a company's brand is not just the responsibility of the marketing department: it's in the hands of all of its employees. Spurred by movements such as social media, employees are ever more capable of building up their employer's reputation or tearing it down. They influence their own network, and are therefore the first base for creating positive word of mouth. When we want to leverage word of mouth, our focus should not just be on customers, but also on our own people. Realizing this, many companies are complementing their customer satisfaction programme with an employee satisfaction one.[17]

We need to recognize that employees have an important role in implementing the customer focus we have defined for ourselves. This starts with understanding the importance of everybody within the organization who interacts directly with the customer. They all have a role to play in delivering the value proposition to the customer, from the lowest on the totem pole to the highest, even the representative in the call centre, often the lowest in the food chain in many companies. But as Joseph Jaffe put it: 'Are you really going to abdicate the last mile of customer interaction, the one where most problems arise, to low-paid disenfranchised workers with zero career potential within the company, no stake in the brand, and an average turnover rate of just a few months?'[18]

Companies that invest in customer engagement but fail to invest in employee engagement lose out on potential sources of incredible underleveraged potential. And they may unwittingly sabotage their own customer-oriented initiatives. When we fail to apply the principles that we use for customers to our own organization, we lose authenticity and strength in our actions. For example, how can we expect R&D people who are the sole owners of new product ideas in the company to accept ideas coming from customers or other external stakeholders? When we cannot collaborate internally, it's wishful thinking that we will be able to collaborate externally. Before you can open up externally, you have to open up internally.[19]

There has been much criticism of companies that reach out to customers through external platforms, but are closed, silo operations inside. What message does the management signal to employees when 'strangers' are invited to submit ideas, but the company's own employees are not? Involving customers is often more time-consuming and resource-demanding than the 'usual way', so managers tend to stay within their comfort zones, control the processes they are responsible for and deliver products and services the way they are used to, having more control over the 'on time' and 'on budget'.

Internal crowdfunding

IBM has been experimenting with 'enterprise crowdfunding,' where the company gives its employees a small budget and encourages them to commit it to each other's proposed projects. There is a website that was inspired by internet crowdfunding websites, where members of the organization could propose projects, and members of the organization could take their $100 and spend it on each other's projects.

The idea is to use the wisdom of the crowd and apply it within your own organization. As a result, there was a grassroots effort, with people advocating their projects across the organization, and all employees having a vote in which projects were going to get realized.

One of the old IBM mantras goes: 'None of us is as smart as all of us.' Internal crowdfunding really uses that principle.

In many cases internal resistance from the company's corporate culture plays a role in inhibiting structural collaboration with customers. The in-company experts often believe the outside crowd has less expertise than they do and thus cannot come up with good ideas. For some, outside collaboration is seen as a threat to their jobs, especially prominent amongst technology leaders whose status through expertise is being threatened by the outside community.

It's often a good idea to start with an internal community before tapping into the world outside the company's boundaries. As earlier examples showed, online communities are increasingly part of the standard arsenal that companies use to connect with customers and to draw in their ideas. The distinction between internal and external communities is the extent to which they reach outside the boundaries of the organization. Companies usually set up internal communities to gather ideas from their employees, but more importantly to foster an innovative corporate culture within the organization and make every employee a part of it. Ideally, a company should have both an internal community and an external one, but run them separately because they have different purposes. While the external agents bring a breath of fresh air into the company, the employees – experts in the field – may get inspired to generate more out-of-the-box ideas themselves, but will also look for the right technologies and ways of making new ideas possible.

However, successful collaboration is not accomplished by just buying and installing an online platform. And the same is true for internal collaboration on innovation. When employees are not used to stepping up with their ideas, and this was not expected from them before, an online community will not suddenly ignite a wave of ideas. People may be hesitant to bring forward ideas that they have not discussed with their direct line manager, or worse, that have been dismissed by their direct line manager. Innovation communities are based on a principle of equality. Everybody's contribution is equally valid, but it takes time for some employees to internalize this new attitude. An online innovation community can be an excellent tool to show that submitting ideas is encouraged, to have a visual platform where ideas can be hosted and discussed, and to keep it going.

In internal communities, ideas are often naturally linked to the company's innovation strategy and process and there is less resistance to integrating them. The difficulties arise from the new processes that are introduced as part of outside innovation. Since the internal resistance seems to manifest itself to a lesser extent when internal employees are involved in the process of outside innovation, an optimal strategy would be for a company to first introduce an innovation community inside and only then one outside of its boundaries. The communities should remain two separate environments, but ideas from both of them should be pulled together for evaluation, or top-rated ideas of one community should be introduced to the other one for feedback. This way, employees are less likely to perceive external innovation as a threat and more as an additional resource for innovation they are all involved in, and so the level of internal resistance is significantly lower.

Build the culture from the inside

To be customer-oriented as a company is as much a behaviour as it is a culture. Far from a marketing gimmick, it's an enterprise-wide endeavour that is as palpable as it is visible. We can build capabilities, data, analytics and processes but ultimately, a lack of customer-centric culture is the major impediment to becoming more customer-centric.[20]

Customer storytelling

So often the informal communication inside a company is only about negative stories about customers: 'Can you believe the stunt X pulled?' 'Did you hear about the impossible demands Y is imposing?' 'We just had a complaint from Z.'

Customer storytelling aims to counterbalance this and change the narrative about customers. Essentially, it is internal content marketing about customers. Successes with customers, compliments from customers, problems solved for customers – share them. How? By creating formal stories about them that can be used in multiple communication platforms.

At online shoe retailer and customer service king Zappos, the core focus is on company culture and the relationships between employees. New employees all go on the same four-week training programme. During this, they go over the company history, the Zappos philosophy about customer service and the importance of company culture. According to CEO Tony Hsieh, company culture is actually the number one focus of the company (and not customer service, as most people believe). You can be an accountant or a lawyer, and you still go through that same training that the call centre representatives go through... The reasoning behind this is: 'If we want our brand to be about customer service, then customer service needs to be the whole company, not just a department.'

CASE STUDY

A very similar story is told by Châteauform'. The thriving seminar hotel group has a core emphasis on customer service and customer satisfaction. But that is enabled by a unique company culture centred on a set of seven shared values. The number one value at Châteauform' is: 'Love for the customer.' Captured and described in a booklet entitled 'Welcome to the Family' (affectionately called 'the bible'), the shared values form the starting point for the culture at Châteauform', a culture where all the company's activities and behaviours are built to maximize customer satisfaction. The booklet includes the reasons behind the desired behaviour, as well as suggestions for the 'how to.' It enables new employees to immerse themselves in the culture upon arrival, as well as to share the Châteauform' way of living together with other team members. In this way, it provides everyone with the same language and helps to bring coherence and direction for employees. Having strong shared values allows for autonomy and trust. CEO Horovitz adds:

> For me, managing by values means, first of all, to have common values. Second, they must be shared or espoused, ie people must identify with them. In order for people to believe, they have to be demonstrated by management practices, they have to be reinforced by the leadership, by the rituals and symbols, and by the reward system. So, everything we do in terms of organization or management practices tries to reinforce the values.

Following the framework in Figure 3.1,[21] customer-centric organizations are managed through their culture because within the organization there is strong consensus throughout on the goal and the actions to get there. A starting point in any change initiative must be an assessment of the level of agreement in the organization along two critical dimensions. The first is the extent to which people agree on *what they want*: the results they seek from their participation in the company, their values and priorities. In other words: what is the overall goal we are striving for? The second dimension is the extent to which people agree on *cause and effect*: which actions will lead to the desired outcome. When people have a shared understanding of cause and effect, they will probably agree on which actions to adopt.

An organization where there is no consensus on goals or actions has to be led by pure power. Strong control mechanisms, clear role definitions and decision-making authority, and coercion through negative consequences are what characterize such an organization. In the lower right quadrant we find organizations where there is no clear goal setting. But even with a lack of shared understanding on where the organization is going, there can still be consensus on the right actions to undertake. In this case, the organization will be led by management tools such as incentives, measurement systems, standard operating procedures and training.

In the upper left quadrant are organizations where there is broad understanding of the goal, but not on the actions that will lead to it. Getting this type of organization to change happens through leadership, by showing vision. Leaders in this type of organization are charismatic, convincing communicators who lead by example. These types of leaders often do not say how things need to be done, they just set the direction. Finally, in the upper right quadrant are organizations that can be managed through culture. Because there is a strong consensus and shared understanding on the 'what' and the 'how', these organizations need no power tools or coercion. They hardly need any standard procedures. The tools to be used are those of culture, folklore and rituals. Châteauform' finds itself in this position. Its strong customer-oriented culture is deeply embedded.

FIGURE 3.1 The framework

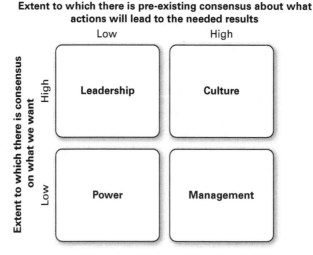

Beware of the BOHICA syndrome

Companies often set up a customer-centricity initiative, and are disappointed if they don't see immediate results. The reason often is that the organization suffers from the 'BOHICA-syndrome'; in other words: Bend-Over-Here-It-Comes-Again.

It means the employees are tired of working towards new temporary goals all the time, they're fed up with the fickle ever-changing stories from top management. And they see this customer-centricity as just the newest thing, before we move on to the next fad. As a result, they do the minimum they can get away with, waiting for it all to blow over.

Building a customer-oriented culture requires time, commitment and focus. It's not a short-term project, but a long-term vision executed across all layers and decisions.

The empty chair in the boardroom

Consider what it takes to compete in retail banking nowadays. Thirty years ago, a bank only had to set up a local retail site with 9 to 5 opening hours to deliver on customer expectations in terms of accessibility. With a well-trained staff of tellers and telephone operators, the bank could cover all requirements of service. Today, you do not even reach the Olympic minimum by doing this. Customers want the bank to be equally available online as offline. Mobile banking has become customary. Opening hours extend beyond traditional office hours. Questions and comments come in through the website, Facebook, Twitter, online chat services, etc and 24/7 availability has become de rigueur.

The same is true in an industrial environment. Customers expect technical consultations, dedicated systems and on-site support. Orders should be delivered JIT, and packaged for convenient handover to the customer's site. All this with extended payment terms, quality guarantees and extensive documentation.

In today's competitive global environment and challenging economic circumstances, companies have to work harder than ever to attract and keep a customer. Customer expectations in terms of product quality, service and company accessibility only increase. The result is that investments in customer service, communication and experience now loom as a larger than ever percentage of total costs. Executives feel that they need to shout louder than competitors to stand a chance of being heard by customers. The knee-jerk reaction in this challenging environment is to shift budgets away from long-term customer focus building to short-term optimizations. Their results are more measurable and fast but they often undermine rather than enhance long-term customer relationships. Investing in customer-centricity often involves making decisions that are financially suboptimal or even risky in the short term, and whose long-term benefits are difficult to prove. Take for example the 365 return policy that Zappos carries or the unlimited budget for service recovery that is applied at Châteauform'. Are these examples of madness or a sound investment in long-term customer relationships? Making sure that these kinds of investments are protected, is the responsibility of the C-suite and the board.

A company that is profoundly customer-centric makes the issue one that is discussed at the highest levels. In many companies, the opposite happens. Customer engagement programmes are staffed by junior employees who have no power when it comes to mobilizing senior people to give them access to 'their' customers. Social media are seen as a tactical tool that can be outsourced, instead of a strategic opportunity to set up a direct dialogue with customers. And marketing, traditionally the department most concerned with the customer, is not present in the power circle in the executive committee. In fact, only 10 per cent of the time in executive committee meetings is spent talking about marketing-related issues. In spite of the fact that over 85 per cent of Fortune 500 mission statements pay homage to the importance of anticipating and serving customer needs, the customer hardly gets a mention in today's boardrooms. Only 18 per cent of Fortune 150 board members have marketing backgrounds.[22] Some non-marketers do have a passion for customer insight and customer care and, as board members, bring this perspective to the table. But most do not. Wittingly or unwittingly, they content themselves with a superficial understanding of the customer, and allow other seemingly more pressing topics to drive the board agenda.

We need to create space for the empty chair at the boardroom. That empty chair symbolically is taken up by the customer. It epitomizes the fact that the customer should have a permanent presence on the board. The voice of the customer should be heard, even if he or she is not physically present.

Walk the talk

In the end, instead of paying lip service to customers, we need to walk the talk. Less talking, more action, is what most companies need. No amount of customer journey workshops will make you a more customer-centric company.[23]

It starts by making sure somebody is accountable and makes it his or her focus. Often this is the CEO. At Amazon for example, CEO Jeff Bezos is known to be the key proponent and driver behind the company's customer-centricity. Other companies have delegated this role by appointing a Chief Customer Officer, responsible for designing and executing the firm's customer relationship strategy and overseeing all customer-facing functions.[24] A successful CCO promotes a customer-centric culture and removes obstacles for the flow of information about customers throughout the organization. To be effective, the role of the CCO needs to be a powerful one, reporting directly to the CEO and with the mandate to enforce changes and not just advise. It's advisable to appoint somebody who knows the organization well, and is able to communicate effectively across departments. Having somebody with high internal clout ensures that the job is seen as respected and influential.

To make the move of appointing a CCO successful, we need to make sure that we are not delegating it away. Appointing a

CCO often means that the rest of the organization spends less time thinking about the customer, assuming someone else is taking care of it. By now, it should be clear that customer focus is everybody's business. A CCO can help to keep the overview perspective, coordinate activities and enable best-practice sharing, but he or she can only be successful when supported by the entire organization.

Walking the talk also means that the company shows it is serious about the customer by putting it in KPIs: making customer focus a significant part of performance metrics. At Châteauform' for example, there is one and only one KPI: customer satisfaction. If you focus on customer satisfaction, the financial results will automatically follow. According to CEO Jacques Horovitz:

> I often hear companies tell me customer orientation is important. It should be part of the bonus of the management. And then I ask them, how much of the bonus is on customer orientation? And they say, 5 per cent or 10 per cent. Five per cent! That means the rest of the bonus is on other things! If you really want it, it has to become 100 per cent of the bonus of top management. The management of multiple priorities does not work. It's a complete shift.

Close the feedback loop

In conclusion, the constant feedback loop with customers that outside-in organizations invest in creates benefits on three different levels. In the short term, the immediate feedback loop fosters interaction with customers, creates customer conversations, and the immediate reaction to individual customers' questions and comments creates a more positive attitude with these customers. In the medium term, uncovering patterns and systemic defects allows you to make improvements. In the longer term, the constant communication about and with customers throughout the organization leads to a more customer-focused culture. This means that there is a triple feedback loop that customer-oriented companies benefit from; see Figure 3.2.

FIGURE 3.2   Feedback loop

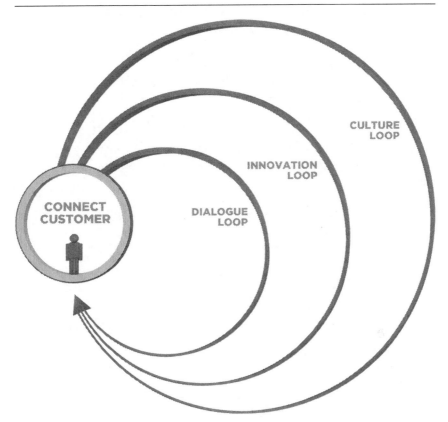

CULTURE
LOOP

INNOVATION
LOOP

DIALOGUE
LOOP

CONNECT
CUSTOMER

3 FEEDBACK LOOPS

In short

- Start seeing customers as key collaborators. Build a structural collaboration with customers by giving them an active role.

- Don't try to solve problems *for* customers, solve problems *with* customers.

- Realize that customers do not only have value for your company in their role as buyers. Customers can also take up the role of designer, adviser, guide, advocate, idea generator and employee. Set up processes to exploit all of these roles to get maximum value out of your customers.

- Consider customers as your top priority in everything you do.
- Go inside-out to enable outside-in. Engage employees in your customer-driven efforts.
- Being customer-centric starts with the people within the organization. A customer-oriented culture is the driving force.
- Make it accountable. The ambition to be customer-centric needs to be translated into measurable goals and objectives.
- Have a long-term point of view. It's a fundamental shift, not a short-term project.

Get started

- Recognize and reward your most valuable customer advocates.
- Invest in setting up a formal customer ambassadorship programme.
- Facilitate the process of enabling customers to be advocates. Make it easy for satisfied customers to share their experiences.
- Set up a customer advisory board.
- Set up a platform to connect customers with each other.
- Involve customers as active participants in creating and customizing products and processes.
- Put customer issues high on the agenda of every meeting at every level within the organization.
- Measure and widely communicate progress on a limited number of key success metrics.

Notes

1 http://blogs.hbr.org/cs/2013/01/the_zipcar_acquisitions_two_po.html
2 http://www.isitedesign.com/insight-blog/12_06/zipcars-principles-designing-great-experiences

3 2010 IBM Global CEO study

4 http://www.forbes.com/sites/kostaperic/2012/04/23/the-castle-and-the-sandbox-how-to-innovate-in-established-companies/

5 http://petervan.wordpress.com/2013/01/08/innotribe-a-tribe-of-innovators-in-the-financial-industry/

6 Lee, B (2012) *The Hidden Wealth of Customers*, Harvard Business Review Press, Boston, MA

7 Taken from the Salesforce.Com website.

8 As an example, read the blog post by MVP Geraldine Gray on 'How to be a successful MVP': http://blogs.salesforce.com/community/2012/07/how-to-be-a-successful-salesforce-mvp.html

9 Extract from a personal interview with Paal Smith-Meyer from Lego, November 2010

10 http://disneyparks.disney.go.com/blog/2009/10/new-interactive-simulated-thrill-ride-opens-in-epcot-at-walt-disney-world/

11 The customer is the company, *Inc Magazine,* June 2008

12 Roggeveen, A *et al* (2012) Understanding the co-creation effect, *Journal of the Academy of Marketing Science,* 40, 771–90

13 http://www.theconversationmanager.com/2013/06/18/new-report-the-self-service-economy/

14 Ramaswamy, V and Gouillart, F (2010) *The Power of Co-creation,* Free Press, New York

15 Heskett, J *et al* (1994) Putting the service profit chain to work, *Harvard Business Review,* March-April, 164–74

16 The company's name will remain confidential.

17 As an illustration, 'employee net promoter score' is a popular new field of application for NPS.

18 Jaffe, J (2010) *Flip the Funnel,* Wiley, New York

19 From Henry Chesbrough, during a keynote address at the Lake Geneva SMS Conference, March 2013.

20 Based on a survey of 72 management executives of companies with over 50 employees, conducted in the Benelux by SAS Institute. SAS White Paper, 2012

21 Adapted from C Christensen, SMS Lake Geneva Conference, 23 March 2013

22 Quelch, J and McGovern, G (2005) Does the customer come first in your boardroom?, *Leader to Leader,* 35, 28–32

23 For an amusing note on how companies only talk the talk, read the Schumpeter section of *The Economist*, The magic of good service, 22 September 2012: 'Phone a firm that has appointed a chief customer officer and see if you can reach a human being. If not, that CCO might as well be tossed from an executive-floor window, no doubt clutching his collection of "journey maps" and "customer archetypes".'

24 Rust, R *et al* (2010) Rethinking marketing, *Harvard Business Review*, January

Connect using the second lens

04

Zooming out beyond the product

The customer rarely buys what the company thinks it's selling them. **ANON**

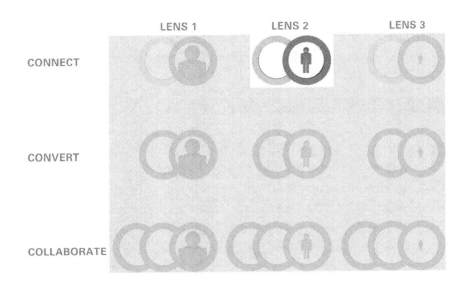

CASE STUDY

In early 2011, Disney unveiled a new campaign for its theme parks.[1]
The surprising part about it? The entire ad showed no Mickey Mouse, no
Cinderella castle, no thrill rides, no attractions, no images of the parade of
Disney characters. The only images in the ad were children getting really
excited, jumping up and down and freaking out as their parents told them 'We're
going to Disneyland!' What was the insight behind the campaign? First, Disney
discovered that across the globe parents have something in common. When they
book a trip to Disneyland they don't immediately tell their kids, trying to avoid
the daily whining of 'How many days till we go to Disneyland?' The moment they
finally let their kids in on their secret, is when the Disney magic really kicks in.
Parents across Europe were asked to film the moment they told their children
they would be going to Disneyland, with the footage then turned into a series of
TV spots on the theme, 'The magic begins the moment you tell them.' The result
of the campaign was a new attendance record for the park.

What Disney realized is that the experience of coming to Disney does not begin
when you cross the entrance gate. It begins much earlier. It also realized that
families do not come to Disney just for the characters, the rides, or the food.
Mostly they come because they want to enjoy family moments together, and
create family memories.

The 'The magic begins the moment you tell them' campaign incor-
porates the two main ideas that form the core of this chapter.
First, we need to consider the entire customer journey from start to
finish. For Disney, that means the customer experience begins the
moment they book their trip, not the moment they enter the park.
Second, we need to consider the customer's latent goal behind their
purchase. For Disney, it is about sharing family moments together.
These two ideas have a profound impact on the way we approach
customer-inspired innovation opportunities and the way we connect
with customers and learn from them.

In this chapter, we introduce the concepts of the customer journey and
customer outcome-driven insights. These concepts help us to look at

the customer in a broader perspective than just from our product or service point of view. The customer journey points us to the fact that customers go through a number of steps to buy and use our products and services. It is by understanding those steps that we can identify the full range of needs that customers have along this journey. The outcome-driven principle forces us to look at our products and services from the customer's point of view, and see what role they really play in the consumer's life or business. The outcome-driven perspective also helps us look beyond functional benefits. What is the real job that the customer wants to get done, and why does he or she use this product to do it? We can assist customers by helping them achieve the desired outcome more effectively and efficiently, with reduced risks and uncertainty. Ultimately it's about giving customers a solution to their problems.

Consider the entire customer journey

As a company, we need to make sure that we look at the entire process of the customer journey, as it represents the overall experience that the customer has with us. At the simplest a customer journey is a linear map of the stages a customer goes through to get the right product and use it for the goal he or she wants to accomplish. The customer journey delineates all of the steps a customer undertakes, and some steps may involve interactions with the company, but some will not.[2]

Let's start from a stylized example of a customer journey, which you can adapt to your own situation. A customer's product search may start with Googling your name or your product category, long before there is any formal contact with your company. A recent study showed that up to 60 per cent of the purchase process in B2B is already done before sales people get involved, and that customers tend to postpone the point of direct contact until later in the purchase process.[3] The next step may be contact with a sales person, and the decision to buy. And the journey continues long after the purchase, as using the product or service, getting customer service and even disposing of the product are all part of that journey.

FIGURE 4.1   The customer process

The exercise of mapping out the customer journey is only the first step. Now the work begins. There are several things we can do with the customer journey as an organization. The first task is to ensure that the customer experience remains consistent throughout. Consistency means that the customer experience throughout is in line with your value proposition. If you're checking into a budget hotel, you're not necessarily disappointed to have to go into the hall to fetch a drink at a vending machine. But when checking into a five-star venue, you will be upset when you do not find a complimentary bottle of water in the room. When you buy a cheap speaker system in an outlet store, you will not presume you'll get great after-sales service, but when you buy the latest Bang & Olufsen, you want the entire experience from the in-store service to the after-sales experience to reflect the same high quality and eye for design.

Second, we need to ensure that we live up to our promises every step of the way. Great customer experiences do not happen by accident. One of the many challenges this customer journey presents for organizations is that different people are involved throughout the process. Siloed organizations will get tangled in the trap of internal company barriers. If your business depends on frontline people such as admin staff, call centre agents, retail sales staff, field technicians, delivery people, installers or other employees or hired agents who deliver part of the customer journey, you have an additional challenge of ensuring consistency in delivering your value proposition along the way. A necessary condition is that expectations are clear. A survey of customer frontline workers demonstrated that 84 per cent said they don't get enough information from top management, while 75 per cent said their employers aren't telling them enough about changes in policies and goals. Almost the same number (74 per cent) said 'consistent' messages from senior management, although few and far between, are important to them, but rarely delivered.[4] Consistent customer experiences require consistent internal communication.

Adopting such a customer-centric mindset throughout the entire company poses challenges, especially for firms with a history of product-centric thinking. We need to start understanding that it is not just the product or service where we need to differentiate from the competition, but that we need to do it consistently along the entire customer journey. If your customer is your top priority, he or she needs to be your top priority in every touch-point you have with him or her. This also means that the customer journey creates many opportunities to add value for customers beyond the main product or service.

CASE STUDY

Consider the case of a glass manufacturer that we worked with. To create more value for its automotive customer segments, the manufacturer decided to conduct an extensive analysis of the customer's workflow, which refers to a logical stepwise approach that a customer has to go through to achieve his or her final objective, with the explicit goal of trying to identify areas for creating additional customer value. This involved identifying a key customer that was willing to work with the manufacturer and, based on the input from a cross-functional team of marketing, sales and after-market service teams, a set of customer-specific needs were identified. Subsequently, customized solutions were offered that not only helped the glass manufacturer secure a multi-year contract with the customer, but was also instrumental in increased margins.

More often than not, the customer journey is seen as a challenge more than an opportunity – a challenge to integrate the multiple channels and multiple parties involved in a seamless and consistent customer experience. Rarely is it seen as an opportunity to connect better with customers and deliver better customer value. The opportunities are multiple:

- to learn from customers;
- to create value for customers; and
- to innovate by rethinking the customer journey entirely.

An opportunity to learn from customers

CASE STUDY

Take the example of 3M's automotive after market division. This division supplies tools and materials to body shops that repair cars after a collision. To understand customers' activities better, the sales force was asked to spend more time at the customers' site, simply observing the workflow. A review of this workflow showed that body shops worked in a three-step process consisting of planning in, production and planning out. The cost structure for the whole process contained four components: labour (50 per cent), spare parts (40 per cent), paint (7 per cent) and non-paint consumables (3 per cent).[5] 3M's products are in the latter category.

It was seeing workers in the car repair shops in action that made 3M realize how to differentiate its spray paint product. It was when observers saw the repair guy fumble with the paint gun, losing time on filling and cleaning it, that they understood that it was not through reducing paint consumption that they could help the car repair shop. It was through helping them reduce unnecessary labour hours by making the whole process more convenient. Introducing a proprietary spray paint system allowed them to reduce the time needed for a paint job by as much as 15 per cent, lowering costs for the car repair shop more than could have been achieved by reducing the price of the non-paint consumables.

Three-minute exercise

When tracing end-users' activities and workflow, a useful approach is an exercise called 'three minutes'. The objective is to learn what end-users are doing three minutes before they use a product or service and three minutes after. We then look at what they do during the next three minutes out in both directions. With three-minute increments, you stretch this exercise until you have a complete view of the entire workflow of a customer.

This approach usually combines interviews and observation. It allows you to see the context and the interfaces (in usage and time) your products and services have with others, so the focused observation is about:

- What products and services are used together with ours?

- What products and services are used immediately before and after ours?

- How well are these products and services seamlessly integrated with each other?

An opportunity to create value for customers

The customer journey is a useful organizing structure for identifying opportunities for value creation. For a company to adopt this view, it is necessary to focus on the activities customers perform while selecting, using and maintaining the product or service in question. We can think of opportunities to add value for the customer by asking ourselves three questions at every step of the customer journey:

1 *Can we help the customer achieve a better outcome at this step?* Considering the goal that customers want to achieve in each step, can we get them closer to it? For example, if a customer in the search stage wants an easy way to compare different offers, can we facilitate that process? NIBC bank created the website www.slim-sparen.be, where a consumer can compare conditions and interest rates on all savings accounts on the market. Châteauform' created an online form where prospective customers can find all cost items in an easy-to-use template to be able to compare offers.

2 *Can we lower customer costs at this step?* Lowering costs doesn't mean selling at the lowest price. We have to interpret costs broadly here. Customers' total costs include acquisition, purchase, usage, maintenance and disposal, ie the costs throughout the customer journey. These include search and selection costs, switching costs, costs of maintaining the product, costs of usage, as well as costs of disposal. For example, companies in the carpeting industry have introduced take-back contracts to help customers to get rid of waste. Customer costs also include non-monetary costs such as time. For example, companies have started to implement predictive maintenance to lower the costs for customers in the product usage stage of the customer journey. OTIS, the lift company, monitors thousands of lifts remotely. Based on the analysis of the data these elevators generate, it can detect patterns and pre-empt malfunctions. This way it prevents failures and reduces maintenance costs for customers.

3 *Can we lower risks and uncertainty for the customer at this step?* We can explore opportunities to create value by reducing the various risks customers feel exposed to when

they buy a product or service. Customer-perceived risk is a subjective measure defined as 'expectation of loss'. The loss expected can occur in·multiple areas: performance risk, financial risk, time risk, social risk and psychological risk. The first three categories of risk are related to the product itself, its price, performance, durability and ease-of-use. Social risk is the potential loss because the product fails to fit the social impressions one wants to convey or project; for example, mitigating these risks by informing a customer about what everyone else thinks help them make better purchasing decisions and so adds value. A simple 'best-selling item' highlight can reduce social risk. A common example of this type of risk reduction is the many recommendation and review sites that have sprung up in conjunction with internet retail. Psychological risk relates to anxiety or psychological discomfort arising from a possible mismatch between the product and the buyer's self-image and from worry and regret about buying or using the product. The old statement, 'You can't get fired for buying from IBM' has been called the most powerful marketing phrase ever created. It reflects the fact that buyers place a higher value on reducing the risk of a wrong purchase than on the potential gains from making a better one.

CASE STUDY

Take for example the ZAGAT Survey, the 'gastronomic bible' as it is called by the *Wall Street Journal.* The family business of Nina and Tim Zagat started in 1979 as a hobby. The venture was based on the simple premise that the opinions of thousands of regular restaurant-goers count for more than the few opinions of professional critics. Thus Nina and Tim built a survey of 350,000 consumers about where to eat, drink and sleep around the globe. The results were compiled in an easy-to-carry pocketbook. This was a unique approach to evaluating hospitality establishments, differentiating ZAGAT from the competition in the short term. Over the years, the ZAGAT brand has become a highly trusted source of ranking and information, helping customers make informed decisions, and creating unique value for them. The company created value for its customers by aggregating the information on restaurant experiences of thousands of people, and relaying this information to millions of others. In product categories where the cost and risk of the experience is high, and where quality can often only be determined through experience, advance information as provided by ZAGAT is extremely valuable. Information-relaying allows customers to lower their search and selection costs and it also reduces the risk of a bad restaurant experience.

ZAGAT is a pioneering example of a business model that now has many copycats online. The idea behind ZAGAT is as powerful as it is simple: people trust information coming from others. Aggregating other users' reviews and feeding this information back to prospective users adds value for them. By seeing what others thought of this hotel, restaurant, store, etc, we feel reassured. The uncertainty of finding the right place is reduced by the service offered by companies like ZAGAT, simply projecting back to us others' experiences. Other companies like Yelp and Tripadvisor have followed in its footsteps and used the same principles online. They create customer value by mitigating the risks of making the wrong purchase.

Players like Yelp and Tripadvisor have exploited an opportunity in the customer journey that was left open by the incumbent players. While the travel industry was focused on their existing touch-points with customers, Tripadvisor tapped into a step where those incumbents were not present: the stage where customers search for information. Amazon, on the other hand, handled things differently by integrating customer reviews on its site. That way, the search and purchase steps could be combined within the customers' own environment, and they do not have to leave the Amazon site to find other customers' opinions.

CASE STUDY

Amazon personalizes its online store for each customer through recommendations, thereby reducing the risk of making a bad purchase. The internet retailer also demonstrates how the benefits of aggregating information can snowball: the more information it accumulates, the more accurate its recommendations – and the greater the value created.

Amazon pioneered the online retail experience and became a global brand within a few years of starting up. There are many processes that underpin Amazon's success, including the all-important recommendation engine that promotes cross-selling. By aggregating data on a large number of customers, Amazon is able to offer high quality recommendations in real time about what customers might like based on what they put in their baskets, or what they are looking at on the site. This approach results in advantages for the customer and the company. First, customers' search time is reduced. Secondly, and more important, the risk that they will make a wrong purchase is mitigated. As a result, the customer feels better served, and ultimately develops a trust relationship with the retailer brand and buys more. The value within Amazon's recommendation engine lies in aggregating and relaying information about products most frequently bought together. The more Amazon knows about the similarities and complementarities among its products through other customers' purchases, the more it can use this information to predict the preferences of customers interested in a particular item and thus create customer value in terms of lowering selection and transaction-related risks. Crucially, a benefit of using aggregate information is this snowballing feature: the more information is accumulated, the more accurate the recommendation is, and hence, the more value is created. Thus Amazon's recommendation engine creates a competitive advantage. It cannot readily be copied by competitors who do not possess the large amounts of data Amazon has collected over time.

An opportunity to innovate by rethinking the customer journey entirely

Breakthrough ideas often originate from taking a broader view on the customer, starting from the customer journey, and using this as the starting point to innovate.

CASE STUDY

Take PatientsLikeMe, the social network for patients with chronic and life-changing conditions. PatientsLikeMe was created in 2006 by Jamie and Ben Heywood. Both had been personally affected by chronic disease. Their brother Stephen suffered from Amyotrophic Lateral Sclerosis (ALS). Along with their MIT friend Jeff Cole they set out to build a way for Stephen to connect with other patients. When somebody gets a chronic illness, doctors capture all kinds of data in their office or at the hospital: blood work, scans, interviews, probes, etc. Then there's a follow-up appointment to see how you're doing. Maybe if it's serious, you get a follow-up call from a nurse. There are the check-up doctor's visits, the tests and treatment. But that still leaves 99.9 per cent of our time spent away from a medical professional's attention, just living alone with our ailments. PatientsLikeMe connects people with the same disease profile.

It now has more than 200,000 patients on the platform and is tracking 1,800 diseases.[6] The majority of them have neurological diseases such as ALS, multiple sclerosis and Parkinson's, but PatientsLikeMe has also been moving into AIDS and mood disorders. The platform is free for patients and offers several advantages: specifically, it facilitates interaction among patients, sharing their experience with various treatments, as well as providing peer support. Each patient has a profile that tracks their self-reported treatment history, and into which they enter the names of any medication they are taking, and note any side-effects they experience. The members of PatientsLikeMe don't just share their experiences anecdotally; they quantify them, breaking down their symptoms and treatments into hard data. They note what hurts, where and for how long. They list their drugs and dosages and score how well they alleviate their symptoms. All this gets compiled over time, aggregated and crunched into tidy bar graphs and progress curves by the software behind the site. And it's all open for comparison and analysis. Information from the profiles is aggregated to provide statistical information on various treatments and medications for a particular diagnosis. By telling so much, the members of PatientsLikeMe are creating a rich database of disease treatment and patient experience. For some patients, learning from the experience of other members with the same diagnosis but more progressed has led to an increase in their life expectancy. Others have found valuable information to take back to their doctor and be more empowered to ask for changes in their treatment regime.

Such is the story of Todd Small, who suffers from MS.[7] The condition is usually treated, as it was in Small's case, with baclofen, a muscle relaxant that works directly on the spinal cord. Every day for 14 years, he took a single 10-milligram pill. 'My neurologist always told me if you take too much it will weaken your muscles. So I never wanted to go over 10 milligrams.' It didn't seem to have much effect, but he carried on as best he could. Small would have continued had he not logged on to PatientsLikeMe. After choosing a user name and filling out a profile, Small was asked to list his symptoms and treatments. He entered the 200 milligrams of Provigil he takes daily to fight fatigue along with the Tysabri injection he takes to slow the progress of his disease. And then he clicked on baclofen, and the website informed him that nearly 200 patients registered at PatientsLikeMe were taking the drug. He clicked again, and up popped a bold bar graph, sectoring those 200 across a spectrum of dosages. And there it was. Contrary to what his neurologist told him years ago, 10 milligrams wasn't the maximum dose. In fact, it was at the low end of the scale. 'They're taking 30, 60, sometimes 80 milligrams – and they're just fine,' Small recalls. 'So it hits me: I'm not taking nearly enough of this drug.' A few days later, Small asked his neurologist to up his dosage. Now Small takes 40 milligrams of baclofen a day.

Aside from the informational value that PatientsLikeMe provides, there is also the emotional value of connecting with others in the same situation. Through PatientsLikeMe people can connect with others who are going through the same thing, and can offer each other emotional support. The site also helps people to share concrete tips on how to live with their disease: how they handle side-effects, what they do to alleviate pain and discomfort, convenient ways to keep track of their medicines, etc.

What PatientsLikeMe detected was a gaping hole in the journey that a patient with a chronological disease goes through. That gaping hole is the lack of touch-points with medical care professionals when people are at home, having worries, doubts and questions. PatientsLikeMe found a way to add value for patients by exploiting this opportunity and alleviating uncertainty along this journey by the reassurance offered by others who are going through the same thing.

Through understanding the opportunities that arise from taking a methodical view of the customer journey, many companies have started to redesign it. Here's a list of questions you need to ask when looking at the customer journey to identify new opportunities:

- Do we understand all stages in the customer journey from a customer point of view?
- Do we understand the problems customers experience at each stage?
- How can we add value by reducing costs and risks along the journey, or achieve better outcomes for customers?
- Are there opportunities to reconfigure the stages of the customer journey?
  - Add stages?
  - Skip stages?
  - Combine stages in one step?
- Can we extend the scope of where we are present along this customer journey?
- Are there opportunities to totally change the journey?

Insights from customers across the customer journey expand the opportunities to add value beyond the product.

Focus on customer goals and outcomes

When we are looking at the customer journey, it is paramount to prevent the tunnel vision that comes from being too product-focused. Looking at things from a customer point of view means that we focus on what it is customers are trying to accomplish with a product or a service. What is the goal they want to achieve? Customers should therefore be asked for outcomes: what is it they are striving for?[8] The customer journey is the path customers take to achieve this outcome.

Consider the 'milkshake story'.[9] Why do people buy a milkshake in the morning? It turns out it is not for the great taste. It is not to satisfy a craving. It is not for the nutrition. What they really want is something to keep them entertained during a long boring morning commute; something that will keep their stomachs from growling mid-morning; something that can be consumed in the car without making a mess of the car or clothes before arriving at work.

Focusing on the goals customers want to achieve helps companies avoid being too focused on the product and the short term. While product features are constantly changing, customer goals often remain the same over time. This is a lesson that Kodak learnt the hard way. Customers were not buying film, they were buying the ability to create memories and share their experiences with others. When alternatives come along that enable customers to get the same job done more conveniently or cheaply, customers will go for them.

Getting customers' input thus should be focused on what they are trying to accomplish rather than what their immediate wishes are for the product. This extends the scope of what we wish to investigate, looking at the product in relation to the whole context of the customer.

CASE STUDY

Take the example of Barco. The industrial visualization company was a pioneer in the projector business and a global leader in digital cinema projectors and projectors for major events. The company embarked on an exercise to get customers' input for a new product line in a market in which it was not yet active.

To get started, it identified the key decision makers in the unit that were going to be instrumental in buying and using the product. Instead of just asking users for their needs, mock-up prototypes were used to simulate a real-life environment, and customers were brought into a setting as close as possible to their actual experience. Real product concepts were validated, instead of having a fictional hypothetical talk about customer needs. The interviews were focused on understanding the requirements of the customer in doing the job that needed to be done. Interviews were done in three iterations. After every iteration, hypotheses and assumptions were adapted and the product concept refined, so that every iteration would get closer to the desired product. What the team learnt was that the solution customers were looking for could not be defined from a limited product point of view. As it turned out, the right customer solution did not involve projector technology, but was about connectivity and user interface. Asking 'What do you want from a projector?' would never have revealed these insights.

CASE STUDY

That is what the story of Orica illustrates. Orica, formerly known also as ICI Explosives, is an Australian-owned leader in the explosives business. The company was founded in the 19th century as a supplier of explosives to the Victorian gold mine fields. Today, Orica is a multimillion dollar company listed in the top 30 on the Australian Stock Exchange by market capitalization, with operations in about 50 countries and market presence in twice as many. Orica still remains active in the business it started in.

How does a company survive so successfully in this cut-throat commodity business? Like many of its competitors, Orica is trying to lower the costs of its explosives to remain competitive. However, engineers at Orica approached the challenge differently. They realized that significant cost saving could be achieved by mastering the precision and efficiency of the blast. They identified some 20 parameters that influenced the quality of the blast and started collecting data from their customers on these parameters. Before too long, Orica was able to develop a prediction algorithm to specify the type of hole that needed to be drilled and the amount of explosive to be used. The calculations are so precise that Orica can almost guarantee the outcome, which led the company to successfully break away from the commodity trap. Orica no longer sells explosives: it is in the business of selling broken rock.[10]

Focusing on the outcomes customers want to achieve allows you to differentiate on relevant dimensions. It focuses on using a product as a starting point from which to do new things for customers that solve their biggest problems and improve their overall performance. Thus, companies skilled in customer outcome-oriented innovation create new value and new growth in revenues and profits, even in mature industries that appear to have reached a plateau.

The scope of our customer inquiry should go beyond the product to the goal the customer wants to accomplish, and in which the product plays a major or minor role. To do this, we need to be experts in our customers' life, processes and business, as much as in our own. Looking at things through the lens of customers' desired outcome has many benefits. First, it leads to a higher success rate when creating new products and bringing them to the market. Second, it increases customers' satisfaction. But the arguments for drilling for outcome-driven insights go beyond successful innovation. They are also strategic in nature and help the company grow.

CASE STUDY

In the mid-1990s, engineers within several GM business units realized that technological advances might enable the creation of a new business focused on the needs of drivers. Thanks to breakthroughs in digital mapping, satellite navigation and mobile communications, drivers might be able to access a collection of information, support and even entertainment services like those the personal computer and the mobile phone had already brought to the home and the office.

GM's OnStar venture started in 1999 as 'Project Beacon'. It married the capabilities of GM, EDS and Hughes Electronics in car manufacturing, satellite technology and customer service technology systems and vehicle electronics. The general idea was to marry wireless communications with automobiles. The prevalent viewpoint at the time was that focusing on high-margin add-ons and accessories could uplift the low margins on vehicle sales. The possibilities seemed limitless for wireless entertainment and information systems, and the potential pitfall of feature creep huge.

But while the technology was there, it was much less clear what customer problems could be solved through an in-car telematics system. Instead of being blown away by the endless possibilities of features, the OnStar team focused on the most relevant role such a system could play for customers. What was the key concern that customers had that could be met by a new product? What did car drivers wish they could accomplish for which there was no acceptable available solution? For Project Beacon that job was to provide peace of mind.

The OnStar team decided to focus Project Beacon on driver security and safety. GM engineers developed a new mobile hardware system and service package. The hardware included a phone, a global positioning system (GPS) receiver, two antennas, a three-button control panel, and a modem. The service offering focused on safety and security issues. In an emergency, for example, a driver need only touch the red OnStar button on the dashboard. This alerts a call centre adviser, who locates the vehicle via GPS and contacts the nearest emergency service to send help. The same thing happens automatically whenever a vehicle's airbag deploys.

Other services include remote door unlocking, stolen vehicle tracking, roadside assistance and remote vehicle warning light diagnostics. That these services really tapped into a customer need became clear: 79 per cent of OnStar customers said 'One of my biggest concerns is having an accident on the road and not being able to get help'.[11] General Motors' OnStar telematics unit has quietly become a profit margin superstar. OnStar currently serves 5.7 million customers in the United States, and 500,000 in China. Analysts peg OnStar's revenues at about $1.5 billion annually, with a margin of 30 to 35 per cent. That's about five times the 6.2 per cent margin from GM.[12] The focus on safety married a key customer concern with an area in which OnStar could develop competitive advantages. Had it decided to offer hundreds of fun applications, OnStar would surely have faced impossible competition from the eventual world of smartphones. As the safety systems need to be integrated in the car, selling it independently from a car manufacturer as a stand-alone device was virtually impossible.

Rethink segmentation

When we take an outside-in perspective, it often requires us to rethink our segmentation.

CASE STUDY

Take Securitas for example. The security behemoth is a global player in providing security agents to business customers. Securitas has shifted from being a provider of temp security workers to being a provider of total security systems. A crucial step in enabling that evolution has been changing the segmentation and the organizational structure that was the result of it: where there once was a geographical structure, now Securitas is organized according to industry segments. Why was this change in the segmentation necessary?

When you think of the Securitas offer as providing security agents at an hourly rate, a geographical segmentation works satisfactorily. The basic offering is the same for all customers, and a geographical segmentation and structure enables you to organize the sales force efficiently. But when the focus changed towards customer solutions, this segmentation proved to be an obstacle. A customer solution encompasses security guards, entrance systems, alarms, monitoring services, etc. Providing these requires a lot more technological knowledge but also industry knowledge. A security service solution for a shopping centre has very different requirements than those for an industrial plant, for example. An industry segmentation was better equipped to take into account these differences. The corresponding shift to an industry-focused organization enabled the company to gain experience servicing similar customers with similar requirements.

The key question to ask about your organization's market segmentation is: does it help better understand users' behaviour? From a feature perspective, different segments might not be very different at all. It's only when we start looking at the value of features, given the job that customers need to get done, that we are confronted with the limitations of our segmentation approach. The prevailing methods of segmentation that well-trained managers have learnt in business schools and then practise in the marketing departments of good companies are actually a key reason why product innovation is a gamble in which the odds of winning are frighteningly low.

Yet many managers give little thought to whether their segmentation of the market is leading their innovation efforts in the right direction. Most companies segment along lines defined by the characteristics of their products (category or price) or customers (age, gender, marital status and income level). Some B2B companies slice their markets by industry; others by size of business; customer segments are frequently categorized more by sales channel or geography and much less so by end user. There is no single right way to segment a company's customer base, but too often companies confuse sales channel segmentation with end-user segmentation. Segmenting sales by channels like corporate and government buyers won't uncover similarities and differences in the behaviour of users in companies or government agencies – telling you, say, which have more sophisticated requirements and which have only basic needs. A company in building products might for example segment its market into DIY, installers, building merchants, wholesale and retail. But basically, the same products are sold in each, and each of these channels lead to the same end-market. To really understand the market, we need to segment that end-market. Only then can we ask ourselves how each of the channels allow us to reach those end-market segments effectively.

Segmenting markets by demographic segments is no better. Having sliced business clients into small, medium and large enterprises – or having shoehorned consumers into demographic profiles – does not lead to a better understanding. The problem is that customers don't conform to the profile of 'the average consumer' in their demographic segment. Often the aim of a company's segmentation is more to identify high-value customers than to really understand all customers. Further, end-customer segmentation often is not granular enough to be meaningful. It is by digging deeper that we can uncover segments where we can have a stronger presence. The question to ask ourselves then is: what makes these users unique? How does that align with our offering? If properly applied, our segmentation should guide us towards those segments that can be better served, and those opportunities that the market has yet to uncover.

CASE STUDY

Such is the experience of Dow Corning. Dow Corning, a privately held joint venture established by Dow Chemical and Corning in 1943, is the dominant player in the silicones industry. Silicone has an extraordinarily wide range of industrial applications, from computers and construction to textiles and beauty products. Dow Corning makes more than 7,000 silicone-based products that are sold to more than 20 end-user markets.

In the years leading up to 2002, the company recognized silicone was becoming a commodity as markets matured. Throughout the industry, profit margins for many mature products had been declining for nearly a decade. The competitive landscape began to grow and customer needs began changing. The company realized it required a more needs-based approach to customer segmentation. A strategic review led to an exercise in customer segmentation which revealed information that created a huge opportunity for the organization. The segmentation led to the discovery that, regardless of the end-user market, customers existed within four segments: 'innovative solutions', 'proven solutions', 'cost-effective solutions' and 'price seekers'.[13] With this segmentation, Dow Corning could easily see which segments it was serving very well and which left room for opportunity.

The Innovative Solutions segment had the most sophisticated needs in terms of technological improvement and would typically engage in joint development with Dow Corning. This segment was a natural fit for the R&D-driven company. The Proven Solutions segment was not so much focused on R&D but needed applications and processing advice. For Dow Corning, with its consultative selling approach, this segment also represented a good fit. The Cost-Effective Solutions segment was looking to decrease the total cost of ownership (TCO). Dow Corning needed to combine its product knowledge with its knowledge of the customers' processes to help this segment better in reaching their goal of TCO-reduction. The biggest challenge for Dow Corning, a highly innovative and service-oriented organization, was to find a way to better serve the Price Seeker segment. This segment knew what products they needed and how to use them, but didn't need all the high value services bundled into the price of the product.

In essence, don't let your segmentation get in the way of customer understanding. In many companies segmentation is leading market strategy like a carriage is leading the horse. Taking charge of an outside-in strategy means taking charge of our segmentation. The different types of segmentation are summarized in Table 4.1 (opposite).

In short

- The key in using the second lens is that you zoom out beyond your own products and services. We zoom out to be able to see what the customer wants to accomplish and how our products and services fit in in the overall picture of reaching customers' goals.

- Make sure the entire customer experience is consistent across the customer journey and lives up to the customers' expectations.

- Using the second lens expands your point of view beyond your own products and services. As a result, it opens up an expanded set of opportunities to add value for customers, changing the role you have towards customers.

- Look at the product in relationship to the whole context and the goal the customer wants to achieve.

- Make sure your segmentation does not get in the way, but enables you to have a clear view on the market based on customer needs.

- Invest in generating insights across the entire customer journey. This includes understanding how each step adds value for customers.

TABLE 4.1 Segmentation

	Tactical segmentation	Micro-segmentation	Inside-out segmentation	Outside-in segmentation
Main purpose	Segmentation to adapt tactical elements	Segmentation to individualize actions	Segmentation to guide sales resources to high-value opportunities	Segmentation to guide new product and service development
Source of data	Survey data	Transaction data	Transaction data	Observation and interviews
Population studied	Addressable market	Current customers base	Current customers base	The current and potential market
Success criteria	Actionable	Completeness	Identifiable	Insightful
Type of analysis	Purchase behaviour and attitudinal data (where, when, who)	Behavioural data	Size and share of wallet data	Needs and buying criteria data

Get started

- Map out the customer process from a customer's point of view. The exercise is centred on five key questions:
  - What goal does the customer try to accomplish?
  - What are the steps the customer takes to accomplish this goal?
  - Can we help the customer achieve a better outcome at this step?
  - Can we lower customer costs at this step?
  - Can we lower risks and uncertainty for the customer at this step?
- Create an outside-in segmentation.

Notes

1 http://www.youtube.com/watch?v=6dpAvdHvwyE

2 Different definitions of a customer journey map are used. Some claim that a customer journey map identifies all of the touch-points a customer has with a company, and thus involves all the moments of interaction. This view is only complete from the company perspective, but it is missing all the steps the customer undertakes where the company is not involved and there is no touch-point with the company. For example, a consumer may have talked to friends and looked at reviews on Tripadvisor before contacting a travel agency.

3 *Digital Evolution in B2B Markets,* Corporate Executive Board, 2012

4 Anne Powers, *Fortune Magazine,* 6 May

5 Muylle, S *et al* (2008) *3M Automotive Aftermarket Division,* ECCH 508-009-1

6 Patientslikeme is building a self-learning healthcare system, *Forbes,* March 2013

7 As told by the *New York Times,* Practicing patients, 23 March 2008

8 Ulwick, T (2002) Turning customer input into innovation, *Harvard Business Review,* January

9 Christensen, C *et al* (2007) Finding the right job for your product, *MIT Sloan Management Review,* 48, 3, 37–47

10 Dawar, N and Vandenbosch, M (2004) Seller's hidden advantage, *MIT Sloan Review,* winter

11 *OnStar: Connecting customers through telematics,* Stanford Case GS-38, 2004

12 http://www.autonews.com/article/20130527/OEM/ 305279958#ixzz2ZISX5dml

13 Xiameter (2006) *The past and future of disruptive innovation,* IMD Case IMD-5-0702

Convert using the second lens

05

Create customer solutions

> *Customers were not buying film: they were buying the ability to create memories.*

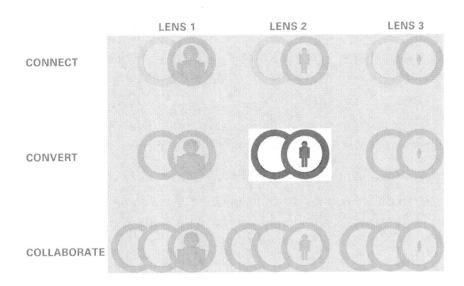

CASE STUDY

Suppose you want to re-dye a stained sweater to its original colour. You go to the supermarket and buy a pack of fabric dye. When you get home, you want to get started so you read the instructions on the package. The first line says that you need coarse salt to be added to the dye when putting it into the washing machine. You don't have coarse salt in your cupboards. Another trip to the shop awaits you… What the dye company offers is not a solution to your problem. It's only part of the solution.

Companies taking an outside-in perspective view their offering as a solution to a customer's problem. Instead of focusing solely on their product, they look at the entire customer journey leading up to the desired customer outcome. It is through this lens that they provide a total solution for the customer, and not only focus on their product's role. Products perform functions; solutions fulfil needs. It's by understanding the goals customers want to accomplish that we can understand how to create solutions for their needs.

To fully grasp the implications of becoming a successful solution provider, an understanding of the concept of solutions is vital. Four key aspects consistently define the concept of a solutions perspective:[1]

- First, a solution is designed to meet a customer's specific need(s).

- Second, based on the understanding of the need(s) of the customer, the solution is tailored to different segments' needs or even to individual customers' needs.

- Third, solution providers should be willing to integrate internal and/or external products, technologies and services to develop an offering that meets a customer's need. Even if you're not able to provide the full solution yourself, you make it happen by getting the missing elements from others. Again, this demonstrates that the focus is a customer point of view: the key element is to provide a solution, not just a product. The aspects of integration and customization play a central role as the different degrees of both integration and customization ultimately characterize a solution.[2]

- Fourth, solution providers offer high-value solutions that adequately solve customers' needs by enhancing customer revenues and/or reducing customer costs and/or reducing the risks and responsibilities customers face.

Providing solutions is often seen as a mere selling approach rather than a profound change in the way the company creates, delivers and captures customer value. Providing solutions is more than bundling together related components. It's also not just a fancy name for cross-selling one's own products and services. The reality is that, if executed well, it impacts the entire business model of the company. In other words, companies need to align every aspect of the business with their customer solution-centric strategy. A number of large enterprises such as IBM, General Electric and Rolls Royce have successfully realized this transition.[3]

As we will show in this chapter, a solution-centric strategy is not just reserved for big diversified conglomerates. It is possible for any company that adopts an outside-in perspective to their offering. By keeping a strong customer focus and working together with others, any company can reap the rewards from a solution focus.

CASE STUDY

Take the example of Betafence. With the industry's largest fencing and access control product portfolio, Betafence is worldwide the number one manufacturer of fencing products. Over the last three years, the company has evolved from a fence manufacturer to a total solution supplier of perimeter security. The company currently employs 1,800 people and generated sales of approximately €400 million in 2012. It has 11 production sites in 10 different countries and sales offices are active throughout the world.

How did the company evolve from the way it did business in the past? It started out as a pure manufacturer of fencing materials sold to wholesalers, the DIY channel and installers. However, increasingly the company noticed that it missed business opportunities. Industrial and large-project customers that are building a turnkey site are not really looking for a fence. What they really want is a way to protect their property and provide security for the people and material inside it. They are combining pieces until they have a system that provides them with what they need: they need a fence, a gate, security cameras, detection and alarm systems, guarding services and so on. As the customers' core business does not involve creating perimeter security systems they waste a lot of time finding out what components they really need, sourcing the right components, etc. Somebody who can take over these concerns from them provides a lot of value – but somebody that's only providing metres of fencing material is facing the commodity trap.

Betafence has started to offer the total system. Their solutions offer the very best in perimeter fencing combined with access control and detection systems. Betafence engages in a conversation with customers to establish their requirements. It helps the customer to define the right materials and holds discussions with architects and installers. It created an engineering department to draw out a complete perimeter security system and guarantee a technically sound solution. It secured the right partners to deliver the products that it does not manufacture itself. It coordinates the entire project from sourcing to installation, and controls and maintains the solution. It developed the technical capabilities to answer questions from customers on the digital access and alarm systems.

Instead of putting a price on a square metre of fence, Betafence puts a price on the total project. As a result of this new strategy, Betafence had to bypass the installers it normally worked with. Whereas before these installers controlled the relationship with the customer, and Betafence was a mere product seller, now these installers provide an outsource service to Betafence. To get closer to customers, Betafence also started its own installation service in countries where there is no mature installers network.

Betafence's value proposition shifted from one that focused on the quality and endurance of the product to a value proposition that is defined from the customer's perspective. It underlines the core outcome that customers want: protection. 'In these often troubled times, the need to feel safe has become fundamental and people wish to protect what they cherish. While respecting the desire for freedom, we offer the protection of everything that people value.'

The story of Betafence illustrates many of the changes involved in going from a product focus to a solution focus. The difference between a product and a solution becomes apparent when one understands the customer journey and the goals that customers want to achieve. When your product only plays a partial role in the customer journey, and only helps customers achieve their goals partly, you are not providing a full solution.

Solutions go further in delivering a complete answer to customers' needs. Solution-centric companies are focused on creating new growth and new value by addressing the hassles and issues that surround the product rather than by improving the product itself. They have shifted their approach from product innovation to solution innovation. Solution innovation expands the market's boundaries. It focuses on using one's product position as a starting point from which to do new things for customers that solve their biggest problems and improve their overall performance. Thus, companies skilled in solution innovation do more than simply take value and market share away from direct competitors. They also create new value and new growth in revenues and profits, especially in mature industries that appear to have reached a plateau.

When developing a solutions selling business, the customers and their business needs should be at the centre of attention. A solution must always be looked at from the customer's point of view. Sales and marketing people need to become customer experts instead of product experts. Consequently, whether a company has a background in services or products, to sell solutions the organization needs to have the customer in mind when designing its internal processes, organizational structures and performance management systems.

In a B2B context, the benefit is that this creates the opportunity to take an expanded role towards the customer, becoming a chosen partner rather than a chosen supplier. To do this, we need to prevent tunnel vision when translating customer insights into customer solutions. The opportunities to add value stretch beyond our own products and services. We need to be experts in our customers' business, as much as in our own.

In the next sections we focus further on the difference in value proposition that solutions require. We also delineate the differences between a product focus and a solution focus.

Outside-in value proposition

Relevant differentiation comes from taking an outside-in perspective, starting from the customer's goals and the current customer journey involved in reaching those goals. This means we need to articulate a value proposition from the customer's point of view. To be successful with a solutions approach, the role of having a strong market understanding becomes increasingly important.

The shift towards solutions is often misunderstood. Many view it as a way to escape the product commoditization they are facing. Indeed, a solutions perspective should help to define the relevant differentiation that customers will appreciate and be willing to pay for. But this is not an excuse to cram services onto products, calling it 'integrated solutions', and expect the manna to start falling from heaven. The motivation to go from a product to a solution perspective can often be summarized as follows:

> We cannot differentiate on the product itself anymore. All options to improve and compete on product quality and performance have been depleted or are quickly copied by the competition. So let's add services to our products and try to differentiate there. And if we obscure the product's price in a total solution's price, it may be harder for buyers to compare prices with our competitors. That way we can maybe protect our margins.

This reasoning is often a recipe for disaster. It leads to overshooting and meaningless differentiation on the services that are added into the product. All this adds tremendously to the company's cost to serve customers, but doesn't necessarily increase customers' willingness to pay. On the contrary, smart customers start to peel away the layers of unwanted add-ons and demand price reductions instead. While the starting goal was to protect margins, the final outcome is that margins are depleted.

FIGURE 5.1 The solution configurator: from disintegrated to integrated

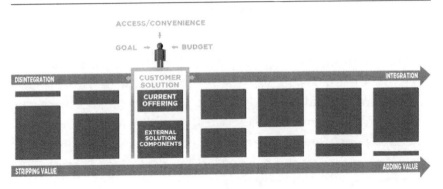

How to avoid this fate? What is wrong with this picture? When the driving force to take a solutions perspective is to protect product sales and find a new source of differentiation, it is clearly driven from an inside-out perspective. And it does not lead to success because it merely means cramming unwanted features and services on top of products. Frustrated buyers are not willing to pay the price premium. They want to scrape off the layer of meaningless features and services to get to what they really need.

To be successful, we need to be motivated to fundamentally shift towards an outside-in perspective, and define solutions from there. Sometimes this leads to additional services, such as when Betafence added installation and engineering services to its fencing offer. But sometimes it can lead to a reduction in services, such as when online brokers offered day-traders the platform to execute their own trading orders without the research, advisory and execution services of a middleman. As we will show in the next section, this perspective can lead to two different types of solution.

The integration solution

Taking a customer solution perspective often creates the opportunity to extend one's scope across the customer journey by offering an integrated set of products and services that deliver customers the end result they are looking for. The integration solution offers a value proposition based on this integration of products and services.

Industrial companies that were originally product-based manufacturers are increasingly adding and integrating all kinds of services into their offerings: financing services, maintenance, spare part management, upgrading and updating services, consulting services, marketing support, training, operations services, etc. Moreover, service-based companies are also entering the field of solutions, creating ties and partnering up with product suppliers or other service providers to meet the needs of their customers.[4]

For technology firms, offering integrated solutions can also be necessary for getting new technology into the market. Due to the complexity of new technology, solutions have to demonstrate plug-and-play applications that make it easier for customers to adopt new technology. Customers often do not have the expertise to envision or implement these applications and there is often no network of partners that have the required expertise.

A company facing such a challenge is Newtec. Newtec is a company specializing in developing and selling satellite communications equipment; it is active around the globe. The company deployed a couple of turnkey solutions for top customers. A main reason why Newtec ventured into such complex offerings, was the fact that neither Newtec nor its partners were able to rely on a network of system integrators, service suppliers or technology partners to implement the complex solutions for them.

These kinds of integrated solutions are not the exclusive territory of business-to-business companies. Increasingly, solutions are also provided to consumers. P&G for example experiments with offering clients a drive-in dry cleaning solution instead of solely selling washing powder. In such B2C cases, the added value created by the solution similarly consists of reducing customer cost, for example by increasing a customer's spare time, taking over customer risks or responsibilities, ensuring outcome quality, increasing convenience for the customer, etc.

Kiehl's, the cosmetics company, offers auto-replenishment programmes so that customers never have to go without their favourite product and don't have to run to the store. This programme combines the cosmetics products of Kiehl's with a delivery service. The degree of customization is the extent to which a solution offering is customized to meet a specific client's needs. Kiehl's allows customers to control their frequency, schedule, quantity and every aspect of their subscription directly on its site, 24/7.

Integration solutions do not have to consist of products and services; they can also be an integration of pure products or pure services. As an example of integration of products, think of your smartphone as the device that enables you to take a picture, share it with your friends and talk about it to them, all with one product that integrates all these functions in one 'fotosharing' solution.

The key element when creating an integrated solution is designing a fully operational solution that will meet a customer's specific needs. The provider takes the full burden upon itself to deliver everything that is required. Therefore, a solution consists of a flawlessly integrated combination of internal and/or external products, services and/or technologies required to fulfil the customer's specific needs. Consequently, each solution is characterized by a degree of integration and customization. The degree of integration is the extent to which products and services need to be combined to deliver a single solution; the degree of customization is the extent to which a solution offering is customized to meet a specific client's needs, as the example of Kiehl's demonstrates.

Four major service capabilities are often present in a solution:

1 *Integration services* – to be a one-stop-shop and to provide fully operational solutions that satisfy customers' needs, the seamless integration of the different product, service, knowledge and/or technology components is an absolute qualifier. In most cases, this entails the integration of both

internal and external components. Indeed, not all of the solution components need to be offered by the company itself. Kiehl's for example works with subscription platform provider, Order Groove. However, even though different components of the solution come from different suppliers, they all need to be perfectly integrated together.

2 *Operational services* – solution providers offer a very wide range of services covering the entire lifecycle of the solution. These can include maintenance, upgrades, customer support services, training activities, spare part management, operating services and so on.

3 *Consultancy services* – as an integrated solution addresses a specific customer need, solution providers support their customers with advisory and consultative services at different stages of the solution lifecycle, from the initial conceptual phase up to the maintenance and operating phase.

4 *Financing services* – these consist of providing financial support to the customer. This can include pre-financing, leasing, or value-sharing contracts that offer financial support during the initial stages of the solution lifecycle in exchange for a share of the value generated later on.

CASE STUDY

Take for example Egemin Automation, a company that offers advanced warehouse automation solutions in different business areas. Assisting its customers to achieve competitive advantage, its solutions focus on improving operational excellence. In the Handling Automation division for example, Egemin offers advanced warehousing and distribution solutions for automatic storage and order-picking of goods.

The solutions it offers incorporate a number of different services. To start with, Egemin supports its clients with consulting services such as capacity calculations, simulations, energy management, etc. Implementing such automation solutions then requires advanced technological integration skills, as these systems need to be interfaced with the existing ERP systems at a customer's site. Finally, Egemin presents its clients with a wide range of lifecycle services, from training on basic maintenance to fully outsourced maintenance services.

Not all solutions consist of all four of those elements. Which type of services to include is dictated by the customer's needs along the customer journey.

Shift in segmentation required

To implement a customer solution-driven approach, we often require a different type of segmentation. Traditional demographic segmentation often is too limited for an in-depth understanding of different segments' needs. As we indicated in the previous chapter, an outside-in segmentation is the first step to understanding the market and being able to define the right customer solutions. The right segmentation also allows the company to really reflect its understanding of customer requirements beyond the confines of what it offers.

CASE STUDY

At Egemin Automation, concept solutions are intelligently positioned by marketing services, targeting specific customers. One of those concept solutions is an Automated Guided Vehicle System for the cheese industry. Not only technical and automation aspects are exploited, but other industry-specific knowledge as well, such as cheese recipes, processes related to making excellent cheese, etc. This all conveys customer understanding and contributes to the unique value proposition that Egemin can bring to its customer segment.

Shift in pricing model

The shift from products to solutions often goes along with a shift in the financial model. Taking an outside-in perspective requires that pricing is in line with the value created.

CASE STUDY

Take for example the securities brokerage pricing model. The stockbrokers' role is to advise clients on the best investment decision: what stock to buy, and when to buy or sell. The traditional pricing model is commission-based. As stockbrokers get commission on the transactions they execute, it is beneficial for them when customers are active traders. However, this may go against the best interests of the customer as sometimes the best decision is to do nothing. In other words: the incentives of the stockbroker and the customer are not aligned due to the pricing model. And customers do not pay for the value they receive. When they would get the advice to not trade at all, it might be very valuable advice, worth a lot of money if it avoids making the wrong decision, yet they would not pay for it. Using a customer-focused perspective requires that the price that the customer pays and the value they receive are aligned.

Going from a product to a solution often means disassociating the price from the product itself and pricing the customer outcome that is created through the solution. This requires innovative pricing models that enable equity between the value for the customer and the price charged. Rolls Royce, for example, charges engines per mile performed.

CASE STUDY

Egemin Automation adopts different revenue models for its solutions. One option consists of pricing a solution as a lump sum to pay once the integrated solution is delivered. Additional lifecycle services are paid for separately afterwards. However, Egemin has also implemented a usage-based model for certain specific, often larger, projects. This is a type of leasing model, which offers the customer the option of paying a fee per transport performed by the Automated Guided Vehicles that Egemin incorporated into its solutions. Reducing the total cost of ownership is then a key advantage for the customer.

One of the revenue models industrial solution provider Atlas Copco uses is a combination of monthly service fees and a performance-based production rate agreement. In a production unit produced per one hour shift agreement, for example, the customer pays a fixed amount. If production increases or diminishes, this cost goes up or down accordingly, as tools are then more or less often used.

Going from a product focus to an integration solution focus

Many companies are struggling to make the move to a customer solution perspective. Why is it so difficult to make the shift?

First of all, becoming a customer-focused solution provider is often underestimated. As a result, it is treated as a project rather than a strategic shift. If it is treated as the flavour of the month, it undoubtedly will fail. Many companies take a superficial approach to the shift. Sales people are trained to become 'solution sellers'. They push complementary products and services onto the market. However, the core products are still seen as the locomotive and services and product add-ons only as derivatives. Instead of really asking what customers may need, we decide for them and push ancillary offers onto them. And as customers carefully vet their needs and watch budgets, pruning all unnecessary expenses, they often resist.

What is entailed in being a real customer-focused solution provider is still misunderstood. It's not a layer of varnish on the existing offer: it is a fundamental transformation of the entire business. This means that there are far-reaching consequences for the entire organization. Product organizations are groomed for products, which is often visible in a product-based business unit structure. These units have their own business plans, resources, channels and customer relationships; status and power bases are built on the units and their products. To succeed with solutions, companies have to turn this organizational approach upside-down: they must question product-focused business practices, scrutinize existing customer relationships, and crisscross established lines of accountability.

The problem is often exacerbated by the company's structure. Knowledge and expertise are often housed within organizational silos that cover only part of the customer's solution. Few companies are structured to deliver products and services streamlined from a customer perspective. Individual units are set up to optimize the economies of scale and level of expertise that come with functional or product-specific organizational units. But they fail to optimize the commonalities from a customer perspective. We therefore need to install the kind of boundary-spanning activities that allow us to bridge across the silos to work together to deliver a complete customer solution.[5]

The trouble is that the very strengths of a good product-focused business can hinder its efforts to become a successful solutions provider. The biggest danger of having a product lens is that it focuses you on the wrong things: materials, technology and engineering.[6] It takes the focus away from the customer. Companies like IBM that have succeeded with solutions, and those like HP that are still grappling with them, have taken some profound strategic actions that go against the grain of existing product businesses. Does having great products hinder solution selling? Not necessarily. But having a culture of great products and a great engineering background can be a handicap in becoming a solution provider. The company will have a tendency to fall in love with its products instead of its customers and its problems.

This dedication to sell products is often at the cost of services that need to be integrated into a solution to cover the full spectrum of opportunities along the customer journey. Services are not looped into opportunities to avoid interference – potentially jeopardizing achieving the short-term sales quota (service sales often requires longer engagement). Sales teams that are traditionally strong in selling products view services as a support to sell products, at most as an extra when we cannot sell products. Senior leadership needs to take action on the incentive system within the company. Assuming that the traditional sales teams will adapt to integrated solution selling without changing the incentive system will not work.

A final obstacle stems from the not-invented-here syndrome. As solutions integrate different components, it will often be the case that the company cannot produce all components itself. Successfully integrating them into one overall solution depends on collaboration with suppliers and partners. Companies therefore need to develop collaboration capabilities that go further than an arm's length supplier relationship. Table 5.1 highlights some of the key differences

TABLE 5.1 Product-focused versus solution-focused organizations

Product focus	Integrated solutions focus
One pricing model	Pricing model adapted to customer value
Product-based business unit structure	Back end, front end, strong strategic centre
Economies of scale	Economies of repetition
Focus on product portfolio	Focus on customer portfolio
Limited number of standardized products for large market	Solutions-specific customer segments
New product or service development	Customer relationship management and solutions development
Transaction-based marketing	Relationship-based marketing
Asset intensive	People, knowledge and process intensive
In-house	Outside collaboration
Cross-functional interfaces	Ecosystem interfaces
Product development -> Manufacturing -> Marketing/Sales -> Customer	Customer -> Marketing/Sales -> Product Development -> Purchasing/Manufacturing -> Customer

between a product-focused organization and a solution-focused organization.

The disintegration solution

While a solutions perspective often requires integration of different components to deliver the desired outcome for customers, the opposite may also be true. There could be an opportunity to add value for customers by disintegrating the existing offer, stripping away some products or services. Three types of customers require a disintegration solution: overshot customers, expert customers, and low-end non-customers and budget-constrained customers; see Table 5.2.

Overshot customers

For overshot customers, a solution often requires one to break down the existing offering into its separate components. Take for example the twist the airline industry has taken. For years airlines competed by adding ever more components into its customer solution (albeit concentrated mostly on business travellers and on that part of the customer journey that occurs at the airport or in the plane). Those components went from food and drinks, upgrades and entertainment

TABLE 5.2 Three segments for disintegrated solutions

	Expert	Low-end non-customers	Overshot
Priority	Specialist requirements Customization	Reduce costs	Increase simplicity and convenience Reduce costs
Offer stripped of:	Integration services Consulting services	All but the Olympic minimum	Features

CASE STUDY

Dow Corning, the global leader in the silicone market, experienced a similar issue when it was increasingly confronted with price pressure. Dow Corning always competed with a full service offer containing an expert sales approach, technical support, consulting and operational services. It discovered however that one segment of the market felt that these services were not, or no longer, necessary. These were customers who mostly bought the same type of product, in large quantities, and had ample experience in using it in their own operations. While at a certain point there may have been value in Dow Corning's additional services that value had dissipated. These additional services no longer really reduced costs or risks for the customers. In fact, because the cost of these services was included in the overall price, they led to an inflated price for customers, who increasingly defected to other suppliers.

To respond to this, Dow Corning launch a second brand, Xiameter, with an offering that better fit the types of costs and risk reduction that this price-seeking required. Within Xiameter, customers can buy full containers of a limited set of standard products at a competitive price. None of the other services is included, and the face-to-face sales approach is replaced by e-commerce. The focus of Xiameter is thus mostly on cost reduction across the customer journey, and not on reducing risk or uncertainty, as the latter are not a priority for this segment.

services on the plane to airport services such as priority lanes. For a large part of the market these services were neither appreciated nor required, adding only to cost but not necessarily to customer satisfaction. In an opposite reaction, low-cost airlines stripped the offering down till only its essential core was left: taking somebody from A to B, fast, affordably and on-time. Low-cost airlines clearly deliver a solution to customers that fits their needs, but not through an integrated full-service solution.

Expert customers

Sometimes customers have their own resources in-house to manage their requirements and only need a company to fill in a piece of a total solution. Pushing these customers to buy into a fully integrated solution is fruitless. They may require a disaggregation of the offer because they possess the necessary knowledge themselves and don't need consulting services, or they have requirements that are so specialized that they cannot be fulfilled by anyone other than themselves.

Customers may also become more knowledgeable over time so they can discern better which elements of the integrated solution they need and which are redundant. When they become educated enough they do not need the knowledge services anymore.

Low-end non-customers and budget-constrained customers

Low-end and budget-constrained customers' priority is to reduce costs. For low-end non-customers a solution may imply that you bring the costs down to an accessible level so they can enter the market. This often happens by outsourcing solution components to the customers themselves. Having customers involved by making it convenient for them to carry out tasks themselves can revolutionize the customer journey by making the desired outcome accessible to the budget-constrained customer.

CASE STUDY

Once, tooth bleaching treatments were exclusively carried out by dentists at a price that put it out of reach for middle-class budgets. That changed when P&G launched Crest Whitestrips and made a professional whitening treatment available at $30. The at-home DIY solution reached $100 million in sales its first year on the market.

All of these types of customers prefer a disintegrated solution to an integrated solution. The reasons are totally different but the result should be the same: disintegrate a total solution into its components and mix and match the right tailored solutions together. Often it is thought that solutions are created by adding on products and services and integrating them, but it can also be the case that solutions are precisely created by disintegrating an existing offer. The key to doing this is to look at the existing offer as if it were an integrated offer, then deconstruct it into its different components along the customer journey. Ask yourself whether every component of it really adds value for the customer or if customers would prefer to reduce costs by taking it out?

To go from a product focus to a disintegrated solution focus sounds simple in theory. It means taking out unnecessary and unwanted features and services that customers do not really value. To do this, we have to overcome our commercial instincts. The purpose of stripping down the offering to its essence is to make a simpler and more cost-effective offering for customers. This does not only scrape away layers of costs, but also margins.

The trap of competence thinking

As already indicated in this chapter, companies taking an outside-in perspective view their offering as a solution to a customer's problem. Based on their understanding of the outcome the customer wants to achieve and the customer journey going along with it, they adapt their offering to fully reflect customers' needs. Their focus is to add value and reduce costs, risks and uncertainty for the customer. When defining customer solutions from this perspective, companies may easily bump into the limits of their existing offering. They may understand the customer's perspective, but realize that to fully deliver upon it they need to step out of their own boundaries.

The customer journey does not stop where a company's competences stop. Taking the lens of the customer journey requires us to stretch ourselves beyond our existing competences. The solutions that customers require do not neatly take into account our experience and existing strengths.

Few organizational theories have had as big an impact and been so widely adopted as competence-based thinking. Developed in the late

1980s by Gary Hamel and C K Prahalad,[7] the concept of core competences is defined as the company's overarching abilities that provide a common theme to its activities. Based on this theory, the corporation is not a collection of strategic business units, but a portfolio of core competences – the company's collective knowledge about how to coordinate diverse production skills and technologies. The concept of core competences is used in three different decisions:

1 *To determine the basis for competitive advantage.* Used like this, the company organizes itself by finding the common themes that underpin its diverse activities. It then makes sure that these common themes are protected and prioritized and linkage mechanisms are built across the organization to ensure that they are appropriately supported and integrated.

2 *To decide how to grow.* Used like this, the company applies the following reasoning to identify growth opportunities: 'Where else could we exploit this core competence?' For example, Disney has used its competence in customer service to set up a new business that provides service consultancy and training to other companies.

3 *To decide what not to do.* Used like this, the company applies the following decision rule to new opportunities: 'Can we leverage our existing competences to exploit this opportunity?' If the answer is no, it decides not to pursue the opportunity. Many companies use this decision criterion to decide on innovation proposals.

It is in the last area that companies may find themselves stumbling when trying to consolidate competence-based thinking with the approach we advocate in this book: taking a customer-focused solution perspective. One may see that the approaches are at odds with one another and lead to different decisions. It is the clash of inside-out and outside-in thinking. If we apply the core competence theory to Betafence's transformation from just fences to providing full perimeter security solutions we would surely never support that decision. After all, Betafence's core capabilities are in steel cord technology and operational excellence in manufacturing, not installation services or security technology. But thinking from the outside-in, it is clear that in order to really provide what customers need, Betafence has to expand beyond the fence.

Product focus can lead to tunnel vision or, as Jeff Bezos, CEO and founder of Amazon, put it:

> The skills-forward approach says, 'We are really good at X. What else can we do with X?' That's a useful and rewarding business approach. However, if used exclusively, the company employing it will never be driven to develop fresh skills. Eventually the existing skills will become outmoded. Working backwards from customer needs often demands that we acquire new competencies and exercise new muscles, never mind how uncomfortable and awkward-feeling those first steps might be.

This quote originates from the 2009 Letter to Shareholders in the Amazon annual report. It counters the doubts analysts had about whether Amazon should venture into consumer devices.

CASE STUDY

Amazon had just launched the Kindle e-reader, and shareholders questioned whether this was a smart move from Amazon, as the company had yet to develop any skills as a consumer device company. Moreover, in this market, it faced tough competitors such as Apple and Sony, both with ample experience in selling consumer electronics. Building on core competence theory, one would indeed conclude that the Kindle does not fit with Amazon's strengths, and Amazon should not take that direction. Building on a customer-focused solutions perspective, one reaches a very different conclusion.

Becoming a customer-focused solution provider requires the firm to rethink its business model completely, to acquire new competences and to seek partners to help fill its competency gaps. These challenges are addressed in the following chapters.

In short

- By converting the second lens into new products and services, we shift the focus from product and process innovation to solution innovation.

- Solution innovation expands the market's boundaries. It focuses on using one's product as a starting point from which to do new things for customers that solve their biggest problems.

- Beware of the danger of cramming unwanted features and services on top of products and calling it a 'solutions approach'.

- Taking an outside-in perspective can lead to two different types of solution value propositions: the integration solution and the disintegration solution.

- The integration solution creates the opportunity to extend one's scope across the customer journey by offering an integrated set of products and services that deliver customers the end result they are looking for. Integration and customization are the key features of an integration solution.

- Moving from a product focus to an integration solution focus requires a fundamental shift in the organization.

- The disintegration solution is based on the principle of a decomposition of an existing solution, a stripping away of solution elements. The market opportunity for disintegration solutions are overshot customers, expert customers and low-end non-customers and budget-constrained customers.

- Beware of the tunnel vision that results from having too much of a product focus.

- Be willing to destroy the value of your existing competences if the market requires it.

Get started

- Translate your understanding of customer requirements into an understanding of the solution customers want to accomplish their goals. Do this exercise for each different market segment.

- Define the solutions components in terms of products and services.

- In articulating the necessary solution components, don't limit yourself to those elements that you can deliver yourself.

- One solution, one organization! Adapt the organization to reflect customer segments, not separate solution components.

- Align the pricing model with the customer value that the solution creates. An aligned pricing model enables a win/win for customers and the company.

Notes

1   For definitions of the concept of solutions, see Foote, N W *et al* (2001) Making solutions the answer, *The McKinsey Quarterly*, 3, 84–93; Galbraith, J R (2002) Organizing to deliver solutions, *Organizational Dynamics*, 31/2, 194–207. Sawhney, M (2006) Going beyond the product – defining, designing and delivering customer solutions, in Lusch, R F and Vargo, S, *The service-dominant logic of marketing: dialog, debate and directions*, 365–80, M E Sharpe, New York

2   Bonnemeier, S *et al* (2010) Revenue models for integrated customer solutions: Concept and organizational implementation, *Journal of Revenue and Pricing Management*, 9/3, 228–38; Tuli, K R *et al* (2007) Rethinking customer solutions: From product bundles to relational processes, *Journal of Marketing*, 71, June, 1–17

3   Davies, A *et al* (2006) Charting a path towards integrated solutions, *MIT Sloan Management Review*, 47/3, spring, 39–48

4   Davies, A *et al* (2006) Charting a path toward integrated solutions, *MIT Sloan Management Review*, 47/3, spring, 39–48

5   Gulati, R (2007) Silo busting – how to execute on the promise of customer focus, *Harvard Business Review,* May

6   Martin, R L and Lafley, A G (2013) *Playing to Win,* Harvard Business Review Press, Boston, MA

7   Hamel, G and Prahalad, C K (1990) The core competence of the corporation, *Harvard Business Review,* May–June

Collaborate along the value chain

Closing the gap

06

Any companies, any businesses, really looking to realize their full potential in the innovation space need to have a very open mind to the types of collaborations and partnerships that are going to enable that potential.

MARK PARKER, NIKE CEO

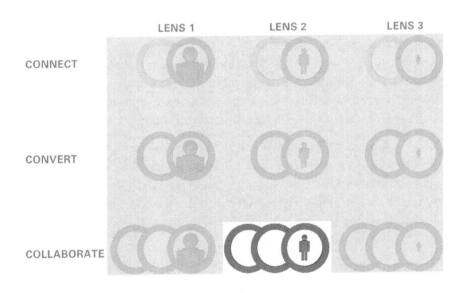

CASE STUDY

A couple of years ago, airline KLM started a deliberate strategy to look at the end-to-end journey of customers. It understood that the flight is not the only service that a travelling customer requires. What they need is to get from home to their destination and back as seamlessly and comfortably as possible. That means there are lot of opportunities to create value for customers outside of the in-flight process.

It all started with iSeatz, a US start-up that organizes all ancillary services for air travel for KLM and other travel companies. In 2012, Your Airport Transfer (YAT), a Dutch start-up, developed an online taxi booking platform together with KLM. YAT has a taxi network in major cities in Europe, the US and Asia. KLM saw an opportunity to enhance its value proposition for corporate customers. Offering the flight and the airport transfer together makes the job for corporate travel managers easier as they can have the entire trip in one invoice from a single provider. For travellers, the service also creates value because they can rely on their transfer and they don't have to queue, worry about delays or overcharges by the taxi driver.

To offer a really convenient solution to customers, the two providers needed to collaborate to create a completely co-produced service. The collaboration needed to focus on seamlessly working the YAT service process into KLM's. To protect its brand reputation, KLM needed to make sure that all travellers received up-to-standard service. A commercial agreement between the two parties described the details of the collaboration, and the due diligence leading up to it ensured that YAT could indeed deliver on the promises.

But the collaboration between KLM and YAT went further than a buyer–supplier agreement. KLM also received an option to become a minority shareholder in YAT. It is a structural alliance where KLM aims at being a strategic partner to YAT and give it access to its distribution channels and supply chain partners. It also tends to act as a strategic coach. KLM on the other hand, as a shareholder, benefits if the company thrives.

Your Airport transfer is now operational in about 75 destinations in Europe and KLM is looking to launch the service in Africa. The service can also be booked via Air France–KLM's Flying Blue platform under the name 'Driving Blue'.

The example of KLM illustrates two key principles of successful value chain collaboration. First, KLM's collaboration with YAT is driven by the desire to deliver a solution for customers. Second, YAT fills in a piece of this customer solution that would be difficult for KLM to accomplish as efficiently and effectively.

Taking the opportunity to create a new customer solution starts with a due diligence analysis of the business model that is required to deliver it. To be able to deliver all of the components of a customer solution, you need a number of assets. These solution assets are the necessary building blocks, resources or capabilities that a company needs to create, develop and market a customer solution. Delineating these necessary assets will inevitably surface a number of missing pieces. You may come to the conclusion that you do not possess all the required resources or competences in house. You may conclude that it will be impossible to take this idea forward because this opportunity does not fit your firm. We discussed in the previous chapter the dangers of this myopic thinking. So the second possible answer is that you want to move forward, but that you need to bridge a resource and competence gap. But how?

There are three options here: 1) you start building the missing resources yourself, 2) you acquire a firm that already has these resources, or 3) you work together with others who already have the resources – in other words, the build, buy or borrow question.[1] More and more, firms opt for the last option. In the short term, it is the option that it quickest to implement; in the long term, it allows them to remain focused on their own strengths and avoid the acquisition curse. Enabled by information technologies that have drastically reduced the costs of coordination, innovation collaboration has become a core element in the growth strategies of firms in a wide range of industries. When they work, these collaborations allow firms to create customer value that no single firm could have created alone.

For the collaboration to work, we have to define the necessary conditions for partners to fit. For example, KLM can work with any taxi firm to set up a door-to-door service, but if it can only deliver in one city this becomes a gigantic task of setting up fragmented contracts with individual service providers. It's in KLM's best interest to be able to consolidate with one provider that can deliver the service anywhere in the world. YAT already had a developed network, which made it a potential partner.

Setting up a collaboration starts with analysing what competences you lack to fulfil the customer's solution. The gap between the needed business model and your current business model indicates what elements are missing. Instead of filling these ourselves, partners can take up that task. Working together, you can deliver the full customer solution.

CASE STUDY[2]

With its total combined annual sales volume of 1.4 million tons and annual sales of CHF4.8 billion for fiscal year 2012, Barry Callebaut is the largest supplier of cocoa and chocolate products in the open market. It operates over 40 production facilities and employs about 7,000 people in 27 countries. Unlike many of its competitors, the company is present throughout a large part of the value chain, from the sourcing of the beans to the delivery of finished products. Callebaut buys cocoa beans directly from the farmer, and produces chocolate pellets that are sold to companies such as Mondelez, Nestlé, Mars and Hershey's. It also has its own consumer products on the market.

Driven by growth in emerging markets and an ever increasing appetite for sweets, the total world chocolate confectionery volume increases by 2–3 percent each year. An additional cocoa bean production of 70,000 tons is needed to meet the yearly demand. In Europe alone, an additional 20,000 tons are needed each year. Over a span of 10 years, more than 700,000 additional tons of cocoa bean will be needed to meet the global demand.

But the cocoa harvest is far from stable. Each year the cocoa producing countries face high uncertainty over the total produced cocoa bean volume. Originating in the tropical regions of Venezuela, Honduras and Mexico, cocoa is now cultivated in a narrow belt around the equator in carefully grown plantations in the tropical rainforests of Africa, Asia and Latin America. Three countries – Ivory Coast, Ghana and Indonesia – grow about 70 per cent of the total world production. For small farms in thousands of African villages, cocoa cultivation represents an important source of income. Because of the political instability in cocoa-growing countries, cocoa buyers are often not fully confident that volume demands will be met. Moreover, on existing plantations, the farmers that cultivate cocoa beans lack the skills and knowledge to improve their plantation's yield, and in most cases the plantations have reached their maximum lifespan of 25 to 30 years. As the yield of the older plantations drops, they become less profitable.

In a nutshell, there is a growing demand for cocoa beans, but global production is unstable and even decreasing. Inevitably, prices for cocoa beans are on the rise. Although Callebaut has the benefit of operating in a growing market with supply shortages, it is nevertheless a market that has its challenges. There is tough competition. Product differentiation is difficult. Any new product is quickly copied by competitors. The big customers are global players with ultra-professional sourcing departments that use their power. This makes it difficult to translate increasing raw material prices into higher chocolate prices.

On the end-consumer market, consumers are more and more concerned about the origins of what they eat. Ultimately, they want to buy ethical products that can be consumed without feelings of guilt. This places high ethical expectations on branded goods manufacturers. An abundance of new certification labels has been brought to market, all confirming sustainable raw material sourcing; the labels include Organic, Fair Trade and Rainforest Alliance. These labels are initiated by non-governmental organizations. Each sustainability label is perceived differently by the end consumer and some are more familiar to the general public than others. Although consumers are bombarded with new labels and can be confused, companies want to demonstrate to them that they are developing a sustainable business in the origin countries, so putting a label on their packages is still considered the most straightforward option.

The four chocolate confectionery companies – Kraft/Cadbury, Nestlé, Mars and Hershey's – are purchasing an increasing number of cocoa products made from certified cocoa beans. As these food manufacturing companies have a strong desire to protect their brands, it has become increasingly important to demonstrate that they are indeed striving to attain sustainability in the broadest sense of the word. However, most of Barry Callebaut's manufacturing customers in the chocolate market lack a direct connection with the origin countries and they expect their suppliers to contribute to the development of a sustainability solution. Chocolate producing companies, including Barry Callebaut, are increasingly held accountable for how cocoa beans are sourced and certified. As a result, most of Barry Callebaut's competitors have begun setting up initiatives related to sustainable cocoa and chocolate production in the origin countries. As these initiatives require large investments, operating costs are going up. So essentially, although Callebaut has the benefit of operating in a growing market, raw material prices are going up and operating costs are increasing. None of these costs can be passed on to customers directly. Margins are under pressure.

To tackle all of these challenges, in 2010 Barry Callebaut launched the Quality Partner Programme for cocoa farmer cooperatives in Cameroon. The programme concentrates on quality farms, quality cocoa and improved quality of life for cocoa farmers and their families, by introducing improved plant materials, training and post-harvest processing methods. Other activities include improving access to education, healthcare and clean water. Being present in the origin countries and having established a direct contact with cocoa farmers assures Barry Callebaut of a constant bean supply, while cutting out costly middlemen. In sum, the programme aims at turning cocoa farmers into true quality partners. By working more closely with cocoa farmers, Callebaut can take more control of its supply, both in terms of quality and volume, and farmers get help in return.

In 2013, Callebaut started training programmes for farmer trainers as well as managers and administrators from cooperatives and other farmer organizations in Ivory Coast. The cocoa training curriculum includes modules on good agricultural practices, post-harvest management techniques, crop diversification, composting, as well as basic business skills and social issues such as labour practices, child protection and other education and health topics. The 'showcase farm' it opened is being used to demonstrate the appropriate use of shade trees to protect young cocoa plants on smallholder farms. Sections of the farm have been planted to test approaches for growing cocoa with other crops including plantain, coconut, mango, pineapple, beans and maize, as well as rubber.

But Callebaut did not stop there. It connected the Quality Partner Programme on the supplier side with a partnership concept programme on the customer side. This partnership programme offers confectionery companies the opportunity to take part in Barry Callebaut's sustainability initiatives centred on the cocoa farmer communities in the origin countries. It allows these business customers to have a guaranteed supply of cocoa beans and products in the future, while anticipating the market demand for sustainable chocolate products. By taking part in Barry Callebaut initiatives, these customers can make good on the sustainability promises they make to their end-consumers. Specific sustainability programmes have been defined with premium customers and, linked to its Quality Partner Programme and the engagement of its premium customers, Barry Callebaut launched its own sustainability label, 'Quality cocoa for a better life'.

Thanks to the implementation of these ideas, Barry Callebaut instituted a new long-term global partnership agreement with Unilever, one of the world's foremost consumer goods companies. This partnership was established in January 2012 and nearly doubled Barry Callebaut's existing volumes with Unilever. It entails a wide-ranging joint business development plan involving close cooperation in innovation, sustainable sourcing, capacity expansion and value improvement.

Connect downstream value with upstream collaboration

As we delineated in the previous chapter, moving towards being a customer-driven solution provider is not a superficial shift. It requires a fundamental transition in how the firm operates, whether the move is to integrated or to disintegrated solutions. This begs the question of how to move forward with this transition. The story of Callebaut can inspire us on the road ahead. It's a story in which we see that value for the customer downstream in the value chain is enabled by collaboration upstream.

The key market trend that drives the actions of Callebaut is the consumer demand for sustainable products. As consumer goods companies are confronted with these demands from their customers, they are looking at their supplier base to support them in delivering what their consumers want. Companies like Unilever understand the end-consumer's sensitivity towards sustainability (Step 1: connect). They are eager to build this into their products (Step 2: convert). But in order to do so, they need help (Step 3: collaborate). In particular, they need help from the supplier to guarantee to their consumers that the end-product they are consuming is made in a sustainable way from beginning to end. For companies such as Callebaut this means that they are under increasing pressure to be in a position to make these types of guarantees. The solution consumer goods companies are looking for is one where the chocolate they buy is coming from an assured and controlled value chain where sustainability throughout is guaranteed. This means that product innovation is less relevant than innovation in the value chain and that chocolate producers need to up the ante when it comes to value chain control. The conundrum is that simply investing in sustainability initiatives only drives costs up, without creating a competitive advantage.

Callebaut went further than this. It cleverly leveraged two assets that are unique to it. The first asset they leveraged is its R&D capability when it comes to cocoa bean farming. More than its competitors, Callebaut has specialized expertise in the earliest stage of the chocolate value chain: growing the cocoa bean. By using this expertise Callebaut can help the farmer achieve better yields and quality. At the same time, it assures continued supply. The privileged partnerships with farmers that it built on the foundation of this expertise create a barrier for competitors.

The second asset is its end-to-end value chain access. Unlike competitors, Callebaut is almost entirely vertically integrated. This means it is in a unique position to connect the consumer companies to the farmer. No other competitor can match this. The collaboration that Callebaut creates upstream in the value chain, with the farmers, thus leads to a stronger collaboration downstream, with the consumer goods companies. Together, they constitute an ecosystem of partners working to enable the final customer solution.

The lessons from this case indicate that Callebaut understood what its customers needed: not another flavour or ingredient innovation, but a sustainable supply chain (Step 1: connect). It launched a Cocoa Horizons department to build the expertise (Step 2: convert) and it set up collaborations with farmers through the Quality Partner Programme (Step 3: collaborate). But the smartest thing it did was to ensure strong customer collaborations by connecting customers within the partner programme. This way, it creates downstream value by upstream collaboration. All together this creates a difficult-to-replicate ecosystem. What we can learn from Callebaut is to make sure that we do not get played out of the ecosystem. By leveraging the assets we have, we can ensure our seat at the table.

Assets with clout

Every ecosystem has a leader that creates the ecosystem's structure, establishes fair standards and designs the reward system for each player. But being the leader does not mean having the most power. Every participant in an ecosystem must ask: 'What is my role in this game?' This is not a question of leading or following, it's a question of deserving a seat at the table. It's also not a question of being the biggest player in the ecosystem. A small player can be indispensable and reap great benefits from being part of an ecosystem if it possesses an essential piece of the puzzle. In a balanced ecosystem, each party contributes some of the necessary assets that other players do not possess. Players with complementary assets work together to assemble the full set of resources required to be successful. Do you need to be in the driver's seat of the ecosystem or can you be in the back seat? For non-dominant players this question is heightened by a lack

FIGURE 6.1 Determine the asset components to deliver a customer solution

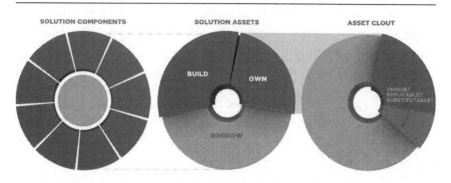

of control. Will I get my fair share of the returns? How long before I'm squeezed out? How committed are the other players to this value chain?

When collaborating with others, there is an inevitable amount of uncertainty. All this depends on the contribution the company brings to the ecosystem. Do you contribute an asset that is required to enable the customer solution? Do you contribute an asset that is complementary to the other players? Do you contribute an asset that is unique? Do you contribute an asset that is easily replicable or substitutable? The answers to these questions determine whether your seat is stable or shaky. You do not necessarily need to be in the driver's seat of the ecosystem to reap equitable rewards from it but you do need to be in charge of your own destiny in the ecosystem, and that is based on an understanding of the assets you bring to the table, protecting them and investing in them. Often, this means opening up the spectrum of the assets you have to contribute.

Defining the assets that ensure your role in the ecosystem

Technology-based assets

When Henry Chesbrough coined the term 'open innovation' and wrote the book with the same name, he heightened awareness of the fact that firms have a lot to gain from opening up their innovation activities.[3] Instead of investing in R&D themselves, they should become better at harnessing the technology that has already been developed by others. And likewise, firms can get more potential out of their technology assets by making them available to others and work together to combine technologies to create new customer solutions.

CASE STUDY

As we mentioned earlier in this book, KLM is working on a new technology-based solution to make the whole process of checking in for a flight more convenient. Increasing speed and reducing hassle at the airport is a key focus area for airlines and airports all over the world. KLM found a solution in using smart luggage tags (cards). Equipped with an interactive display, the card will show the passenger relevant information about their flight. When checking in for your next flight, information is recorded onto the card so that the customer has all information in one place. The customer can also access the KLM lounge with the same card. The smart card is linked to your bag so the system makes sure they travel together.

To realize this idea, KLM is working with Fast Track Company, a start-up technology company. The project is being realized with the help of the Mainport Innovation Fund – reserved for innovative partnerships and for support of start-ups with innovative technologies in aviation. Fast Track Company fits very well with KLM's self-service strategy. By integrating an active matrix display into a smart card, Fast Track Company makes it possible to view tickets, boarding passes, bag tags, frequent flier card info and all other relevant information in a secure and controlled environment that is always with the customer. With a permanent label you don't have to tag your bag every time you travel. The tag is barcoded, as well as RFID enabled, so its use is flexible. For KLM the greatest benefit of this new solution is the time saving for the customer – 30 per cent of drop-off time is spent on tying labels around bags – and also the cost savings from self-service drop-off units. By using the Fast Track Company smart cards and tags, customers will pass faster through the airport and will no longer have to label their baggage every time they travel. For KLM, it is crucial that the technology is backward-compatible with conventional barcode scanning technology. This way, it can also benefit from increased operational efficiencies.

For KLM, it makes perfect sense to use the technology developed by Fast Track Company as it possesses a unique technology that would be virtually impossible (and too resource-consuming) for KLM to develop itself. Why not tap into the technology that somebody else has already developed? But as the story shows, it goes further than simply acquiring technology. To make it effective, Fast Track Company and KLM need to collaborate to make sure their technologies are compatible with each other and can be integrated in a single customer solution. To solidify the relationship, KLM became an investor in Fast Track Company. This assures them that there will be goal alignment. More than acquiring technology, what KLM does is marry innovation processes. For Fast Track Company, this is a perfect example of how technology assets can ensure a company's role in the value chain.

The assets that a company can contribute to an ecosystem go further than just technology. The examples from Callebaut and KLM and YAT illustrate that the spectrum is much broader. Callebaut indeed exploited its R&D prowess but it did so mostly by creating an educational programme for the farmer communities and setting up partnerships through which these farmers can benefit from Callebaut's R&D, not by directly using that R&D itself. It also exploited its access to the farmer communities by giving the consumer chocolate companies the opportunity to buy into these programmes. KLM, in its collaboration with YAT, was not after YAT's technology. It needed the network that YAT can provide.

Aside from technology-based assets, market-based assets provide a powerful basis for growth. Market-based assets can be categorized according into three different types: data-based, access-based and experience-based assets.

Experience-based assets

A customer experience competence consists of the resources required to serve certain customers: understanding of their needs and buying process, access to sales and distribution channels, brand and firm reputation in the market, and communication channels.[4]

A typical example is the collaboration between big pharma companies and smaller biotech firms, such as the recent venture between

Thrombogenics and Alcon, a Novartis daughter, for the worldwide distribution and sales of its eye drug Jetrea. Biotech companies co-develop their drug candidates with downstream pharmaceutical companies holding the complementary marketing capabilities to bring a new drug to the market. In the collaboration, small drug development companies contribute their research assets, and big established pharmaceutical companies contribute their market access assets. Together, they can successfully develop and market new drugs, whereas alone they would lack critical resources. The combination of R&D assets on the one hand and customer experience assets on the other hand is like a yin and yang system.

CASE STUDY

Experience-based assets can be leveraged in different ways than just creating access to a market. Take the example from Carglass. Carglass Belgium, a subsidiary of one of Europe's leading automotive glass fitting companies, recognized that customer service was the single most important factor in both retaining existing customers and winning new business. This was based on a fundamental belief in the power of positive word-of-mouth. Although an individual customer may not need a new windscreen every year, it's quite likely that he or she will know someone who does. If Carglass can get him or her to recommend Carglass to friends and colleagues, it has an advantage over competitors.

Surveys are conducted by a third-party organization, which sends online questionnaires to customers after they have visited a Carglass site. The answers are used to calculate the NPS (Net Promoter Score[5]) for each customer, rated from −100 to +100. Carglass's customer solutions team calls every person who gave a low score to find out why the score is low, and what the company can learn from it. Results are fed back to the staff at each service location, who receive their personal scorecard on a weekly basis. The entire system is a powerful information source that allows it to make continuous improvements to its service and install a customer-focused culture.

But Carglass found a way to make its NPS report work even more. A significant part of customers come to Carglass upon recommendation of their insurance broker. Without this channel, Carglass would lose an important source of customers. To ensure the collaboration of the insurance broker, Carglass sales people regularly visit them to inform them about the unique aspects of the Carglass service. Their task is difficult though, as they do not have anything tangible to offer in return for the positive recommendations from insurance brokers. That is until Carglass realized it had access to a unique asset that is also of interest to the insurance broker: the NPS report of their customers. The NPS scores had only been used by Carglass internally; now, it starts using them externally. Carglass set up a programme that teaches insurance brokers about the NPS system and its value. It also talks about its NPS scores; this way it reassures the insurance brokers that if they send their customers to Carglass, they will be happy with the service they receive. Even more, it gives the insurance brokers access to personalized reports about its customers. By doing this, it leverages a unique asset and uses it to create personalized value for the insurance broker. As a result, brokers are more likely to refer to Carglass.

Access-based assets

Access-based assets are based on the company having privileged access to a critical resource or customer base.

CASE STUDY

Earlier in the book we introduced OnStar, the GM subsidiary that provides in-vehicle security, navigation, remote diagnostic and emergency services to more than 6 million subscribers. The initial distribution strategy for OnStar quickly emerged as a major stumbling block. At launch, OnStar was designated for standard installation on just one model, the 1997 Cadillac DeVille. As with other add-on amenities like DVD players and rear spoilers, this meant that the Cadillac dealer would be responsible for selling, installing and briefing the customer about OnStar. Unfortunately, the cost of OnStar made it a relatively unattractive proposition for most dealers. OnStar cannot be installed easily into a new vehicle: it must be connected to many of the car's electronic components, from airbags to diagnostic sensors to door locks and headlights, and cannot be sold separately from the car like other accessories.

In early 1999, GM's leadership made two tough choices. One was to make OnStar a factory installed option on a wide array of new GM vehicles, not just on Cadillacs. Factory installation would allow GM to leverage its one significant advantage in building a mobile services business: its unique access to the huge installed base of GM produced vehicles. The other choice was to make OnStar available to other carmakers. The idea behind this was to make OnStar the de facto standard of the newly emerging in-vehicle services business. Today, OnStar is available on cars made by Lexus (Toyota's luxury brand), Audi, Acura, Isuzu and Subaru, with more automakers coming online every year. In combination, these moves produced a dramatic growth explosion for OnStar.

The crucial factors in GM's success have been its ability to look at customers' driving needs from a fresh perspective and its decision to serve these needs through a business design that leverages GM's unique asset – its unequalled base of vehicles. OnStar grew by leveraging the brand and the installed base by in-factory installation and by offering a platform for others to tap into.

Access can go so far as creating customer lock-in when the company owns a critical resource that is valuable for customers. Data can be such a resource.

Data-based assets

By leveraging data-based assets, the company utilizes unique data it has at its disposal. These data are often a natural by-product of operating its business. But used well, they can be exploited to create value for customers that is difficult to replicate by others.

CASE STUDY

Take for example Connecticut-based Otis Elevators. It is the world's largest manufacturer and operator of lifts, escalators and moving walkways. The company was founded in 1853 and grew to serve more than 200 national markets generating revenue of $12.4 billion in 2011.

The core revenue stream in the elevator industry is the servicing of installed equipment. Over the years and due to the development of elevator technology, the elevator and escalator markets have become quite mature in providing this basic service. To stay ahead of the game in an increasingly commoditized market, Otis had to look for new opportunities. The company decided to focus on metrics such as minimizing out-of-service time and on goals such as automating the maintenance procedures of lifts. As part of this initiative, Otis developed a sophisticated remote monitoring system. Its monitoring software continuously scans up to 325 different elevator components seeking anomalies and detecting any deteriorating components so that they can be preventatively replaced. But from our perspective, what is of interest is that Otis Elevators recognized the potential for aggregating elevator data to predict future breakdowns and faults. At any given time, the system is gathering and collating information from thousands of elevators. If a similar malfunction is detected in a number of lifts, Otis can issue a corrective instruction for all lifts that might develop a similar defect and technicians are dispatched to replace problem components. Customers are not only spared the time and effort required to book a regular maintenance check, but the risk of an unexpected elevator breakdown is significantly reduced as well.

Interestingly, the more history the business has in producing these predictions, the more accurate they tend to be, and hence the more valuable they are. We introduced earlier in the book the example of Orica, the company that uses a mathematical model to fine-tune the amount of explosives needed for a blast. Orica and Otis gather data to be able to predict future events; size and nature of blast for Orica, elevator breakdowns for Otis Elevators. The insights from the data are utilized within the company, but are transformed later into a direct customer benefit, such as trust and assurance, or cost savings.

CASE STUDY

Komatsu is using a similar approach. Komatsu is an international industrial equipment manufacturer, headquartered in Tokyo. As one of its activities, it sells and services mining equipment for use in mines such as the

Minera Los Pelambres mine. This copper mine is located about 240 kilometres northeast of Santiago in Chile. The world's sixth largest copper mine, it produces more than 400,000 tons each year. Komatsu is responsible for all dump trucks in this mine under a full-maintenance contract. Dump trucks are absolutely critical to mining operations so assuring their availability is crucial as the work in the mine is halted if the dump trucks are not operational.

The mining equipment has a variety of sensors that transmit information and alerts. Komatsu believed that it could utilize this information more effectively, engage in proactive maintenance and thereby improve machine availability. Komatsu set up the Vital Signs Project. The term 'vital signs' originally comes from medicine, implying pulse, blood pressure and other signs to diagnose human health conditions. The data and information coming from the machines is comparable to the vital signs of the human body, giving an overview of the state of the equipment. Under the Vital Signs Project, Komatsu is keeping a database of the causes, urgency and importance of information on vital signs transmitted from the mining equipment, as well as necessary countermeasures. By using this database, Komatsu can provide more timely and accurate product support, and thereby further enhance machine availability.[6]

In the past, when maintenance crews received alerts, they looked for hints at the mine site, asking mechanics, workers and planners on jobsites for further information. All this took time away from their core job. Today, the Vital Signs database helps them to identify the most critical vital-sign data and to develop customized reports with simple but reliable recommendations. But they can go further than this. More specifically, Komatsu has improved preventive maintenance through the better use of backlogs and pre-maintenance reports. It has also developed proactive maintenance by analysing new failure modes and by eliminating or mitigating their impact.

The whole project was developed in close collaboration with the customer and the site workers. The main reason for this was to break the inertia of doing things the same way the customer's employees did for years. Komatsu tackled this problem by encouraging participation and giving 'visibility' at all levels of the customer's organization.

The example of Komatsu shows that we can go beyond the idea of preventative maintenance. By actively using data to fine-tune and optimize maintenance and repair schedules and prevent malfunctions, Komatsu creates a lot of value for customers. More important, by using the data in proprietary prediction models it creates an asset whose value accumulates over time and that is difficult for competitors to copy.

In an era of so-called 'big-data', many companies realize that they possess information that can be turned into value. Often, this information already exists but nobody appreciated that it could be valuable. It's like a hidden treasure in the attic. But data themselves are useless if not turned into knowledge that creates value for customers. For example, Komatsu and Otis only create a competitive advantage and customer value by developing a predictive model, not by just summarizing the data available. Moreover, to unlock the potential of information we have, it is often necessary to combine different sources of information from different areas in the company.

What asset cocktail can you mix?

Combining different types of assets can create a cocktail that becomes almost impossible for competitors to imitate. For example, knowing specific information about your customers and using it to their benefit can create a voluntary customer lock-in effect. This occurs because of the trust developed between the customer and the company, such as with Otis Elevators and Orica, but also simply due to the effect of cumulative data collection over a period of time.

CASE STUDY

To illustrate, consider Netflix, the online movie rental company with its innovative recommendation engine Cinematch. Cinematch is Netflix's engine for collaborative filtering, designed to ask every user after they have returned a movie, to rate it on a five-point scale. Based on this simple rating mechanism, Netflix's machine learning algorithm senses the user's profile over time and matches it against profiles of other customers to look for similar movie-watching profiles. There is a complex algorithm behind the recommendation engine, but all in all, it is based purely on a mathematical formula, and theoretically can be reverse-engineered.[7]

So what makes Netflix the best-rated and by far the largest and fastest-growing movie and streaming company in the world serving more than 23 million members in the United States, Canada and the United Kingdom? Clearly, Netflix's big strength is the data advantage it has accumulated as a first mover in collaborative filtering in the movie industry. By accumulating over 2 billion movie ratings over the years, Netflix's Cinematch is able to generate recommendations with such precision that it would be difficult for rivals to replicate. And the system gets smarter with every additional movie rating, so the accuracy of recommendations increases as we speak, leading to accumulating competitive advantage. Today recommended titles make up 60 per cent of the customers' wish lists.

The fact that Netflix's customers appreciate the company's services and recommendations is illustrated by the consistently low churn rate and an NPS of 94 per cent. Moreover, customers tend to get more value from their relationship with Netflix the longer they use the service. Every time they are asked to rate a movie, the system gets to know their preferences and so creates better recommendations. This inevitably creates a voluntary lock-in effect – who would give up their ratings of some 200 movies in return for a dollar saved on a subscription with the competition?

But the advantage of Netflix reaches further than its recommendation system. Netflix has an impressive catalogue of movies and other content that it can offer to customers. Analysts estimate that Netflix's content library, at more than 60,000 titles, is roughly double to triple the size of Amazon's. Competitors are struggling to offer the same amount of content. Netflix's catalogue size thus is an important asset, as is its recommendation algorithm. But the combination of both offers much more value to customers than the sum of their individual value. Imagine having to browse through thousands of movies without any guidance on finding anything similar to what you already liked. It would leave you bewildered, and choosing only the most obvious choices. The value of having a lot of choice would be greatly diminished. Now imagine getting personal recommendation on a small catalogue. It's nice, but probably you would have been able to navigate your own way through the limited set of options. The point is that the value of the large catalogue or the recommendation engine individually is not so big. But the combination of both offers a lot of value. It is also the combination of the size of this library and the recommendation algorithm together that is virtually impossible for competitors to match. The more complementary assets we can combine, the stronger the competitive advantage we develop.[8]

Complementary assets increase each other's value. The value of two assets together becomes higher than the sum of their individual value. That means to replicate the same value, it is necessary to replicate both components together. The imitation barrier is higher because a competitor needs to replicate the entire system, not just individual elements to reach the same result.

Recreate the value chain

As part of creating collaboration across the value chain, it is often necessary to rethink the value chain itself and who to partner with. By disintermediation, companies jump forward in the value chain and cut out an intermediary. By intermediation, the opposite happens: companies create a new intermediary in the value chain. Both phenomena can be the result of driving new customer solutions through the value chain, or can be necessary to enable new customer solutions.

Disintermediation

A range of intermediaries often stand between you and your end customer or user. Distributors, sales people, retailers, wholesalers, etc all are closer to the customer in the value chain. This can be a major stumbling block in bringing new customer solutions to the market. For many companies, offering solutions to the customer entails moving downstream in the value chain.

In the previous chapter we introduced the idea of integration and disintegration solutions. Both types often lead to disintermediation, but the process and rationale leading up to it are different. An integration solution often contains products and services. It often requires a high degree of collaboration between vendor and customer. Consequently, to move downstream, controlling the channels to the customer is vital. To be able to deliver the solution to customers, companies have to be in control of the customer relationship directly and this means cutting out the middleman. While this may lead to backlash in the short term from intermediaries who feel bypassed, in the long term it is a necessary evil. Short-circuiting the intermediaries is the collateral damage of an integrated solutions strategy. For Betafence, for example, moving towards being a solution provider meant breaching the exclusive collaboration with its installer base. While this was difficult to explain at first, in the long term it proved to be the win-win choice: the strategy made it possible to obtain larger projects of higher complexity. The value for Betafence-installers where Betafence takes the lead has more overall potential than where the installer takes the lead with the customer.

The complexity of integration solutions also represents an opportunity for solution providers to position themselves more downstream and create value by managing the combination of the products and services required.[9] As customers are in favour of reducing the number of parties they need to do business with, the solution provider positions itself as a preferred partner and one-stop-shop. For that, you need to get the mandate from the customer to take on a bigger role than before. You need to be seen as more than a component provider, more than a product-focused company. When a company positions itself as a solution provider, an expert in the customer's business, it is better able to grasp that opportunity.

A disintegration solution also often leads to disintermediation. Customers for a disintegration solution want stripped-down, cheaper and more convenient offerings. Stripped-down offerings for expert customers often do not require the consultative sales approach that intermediaries provide, but can be sold directly. Low-end and budget-constrained customers' priority is to reduce costs. Cheaper offerings are made possible partly by removing the extra layers of intermediaries and passing their margins onto the customer. More convenient offerings require simple, convenient, direct channels. In the previous chapter, we discussed the example of Dow Corning and Xiameter: through Xiameter, Dow Corning offered a direct e-commerce channel to its customers, bypassing internal and external intermediaries.

Intermediation

As with disintermediation, intermediation can also be the enabler of new customer solutions. A great example that illustrates this principle is the Bongo box.

CASE STUDY

The Bongo box was designed to enable consumers to give an experience to each other. An experience cannot be easily packaged to serve as a gift, unlike a product. Bruno Spaas and Mark Verhagen solved that problem when they started the Bongo experience box as a spin-off of their hotel booking site Weekendesk. The Bongo box offered these experiences in a stylish cardboard box, complete with an accompanying booklet that described the various options included. The recipient of a box could browse through the various options and select one of them. Each box centred on one particular kind of experience. For example, the 'Helicopter flight' box was listed in the Adventure category, and offered different kinds of helicopter flights at several different locations. The recipient of the gift chose which option he or she liked best, and then cashed in the gift via the Bongo booking website or contacting the provider directly.

Launched in 2003, the Bongo box was an immediate hit and took off like a rocket. It solved the eternal issue that all of us experience around Christmas or other times of celebration: what on earth to give my nephew/aunt/acquaintance/colleague? By giving the recipient flexibility, the giver does not have to commit to a certain choice. And the thematic boxes offer a bit more personalization than an anonymous gift voucher. Clearly the value proposition of the Bongo box had struck a chord with consumers.

But in essence, Bongo did not create any new product. All of the experiences provided through the boxes already existed, and were available directly from the service provider. Bongo positioned itself merely as an intermediary, repackaging existing offerings. By taking this position as an intermediary between service providers and people searching for a gift, Bongo created a dual value proposition that worked for both. For consumers, the value proposition is a convenient gift; for service providers, it is a sales channel through which to sell extra capacity and gain awareness and access to new customers. Bongo thus functions as a platform that creates a new value proposition in the gift business by grouping and recombining the offers of different service providers and repackages it to offer to consumers.

Bongo provides an example of a platform business model. A platform leader works with the companies supplying complementary products and services and together they form an ecosystem that can greatly increase the value of their individual offerings as more customers adopt the platform.[10] As more consumers buy Bongo boxes, it becomes a more valuable channel for service providers to resell their offerings through. Platform business models create an intermediary between companies and customers. Google, for example, is an intermediary between advertisers and internet users through its search engine.

A common type of platform business model is one where the platform provider not only connects providers and users but also offers a core product that is combined with the providers' products and services. This core product's value is then enhanced through the complementary products and services that providers offer through the platform. For example, the iPhone functions as a platform for app developers to reach their users. This type of platform also contains network effects. The more users on the platform, the more sense it makes to offer the complementary products and services through the platform. As more and more smartphone users are on the Android platform, it becomes paramount for app developers to also be android-compatible.

Often, there are also secondary network effects in the platform business model, which happen between users. They occur when the value of the platform for the user increases as more users adopt it. For example, the more people use Facebook, the more value for other users. Indeed, as the essence of social media is to share with others, it makes no sense to be the only user.

In short

- An outside-in value proposition means that we completely take the customer's perspective on their needs. Invariably companies are confronted with the boundaries of what they can deliver themselves. It is almost impossible for one company to have all the elements in-house to deliver the customer solution that the market demands. Instead of trying to fill in the missing pieces yourself, close the gap between the as-is and should-be by collaborating with others.

- Keep your eye on the ball: the goal is to deliver a customer solution, not to leverage your existing assets.

- Solution components translate into solution assets: the necessary resources and capabilities that are required to create and deliver a customer solution. You may already own some of those assets; others need to be built or borrowed from other players.

- To deserve a seat at the table, any company participating in a solution-driven business model needs to be able to contribute valuable assets.

- The ability of a company to capture value from a solution depends on the clout its assets have. Powerful asset cocktails combine uniqueness with complementarity, creating a system that is hard if not impossible for competitors to imitate.

- To deliver customer solutions, be prepared to rethink the value chain to the customer.

Get started

- Develop a clear view on the individual solution components.

- Do a due diligence analysis of the solution assets that are required to bring a customer solution to the market.

- Categorize solution assets in the own/build/borrow categories by answering the following questions:
  - What solutions assets do we currently own?
  - What solution assets have a complementarity effect to the owned assets? If possible, build those assets. If building is not possible or too slow, collaborate with asset owners and carefully manage asset integration.
  - What solution assets have no additional complementarity effect to the owned assets? Borrow those assets by collaborating with others that already own them.
- Assess the individual and combined clout of complementary assets to understand the value-capturing potential you have in the ecosystem.

Notes

1 Capron, L and Mitchell, W (2012) *Build, Borrow, or Buy*, Harvard Business School Press, Boston, MA

2 ECCH case 513-072-1, 2013

3 Chesbrough, H W (2003) *Open Innovation: The new imperative for creating and profiting from technology*, Harvard Business School Press, Boston, MA

4 Danneels, E (2002) The dynamics of product innovation and firm competence, *Strategic Management Journal*, 23, 1095

5 Net Promoter Score: the difference between the number of promoters, ie customers who are most likely to create a positive word-of-mouth for a company by promoting its products and/or services to other people and the number of detractors, ie people who are likely to create a negative word-of-mouth for a company by discouraging other people from buying products and/or services, expressed as a percentage of the total customer base. NPS is based on the results of a company's satisfaction survey.

6 This example was taken from http://www.komatsu.com/CompanyInfo/ir/annual/html/2012/special/Chile/

7 Gallaugher, J M (2008) Netflix case study: David becomes Goliath, www.gallaugher.com, viewed at: http://www.gallaugher.com/Netflix%20Case.pdf, on 03 May 2011

8 Complementary assets are assets whose combined value is bigger than the sum of their individual values. For further reading on asset complementarities see Porter, M and Siggelkow, N (2008) Contextual interactions within activity systems and sustainability of competitive advantage, *Academy of Management Perspectives,* 22, 2, 34–56

9 Davies, A *et al* (2006) Charting a path toward integrated solutions, *MIT Sloan Management Review,* spring, 39–49

10 Gawer, A and Cusumano, M (2008) How companies become platform leaders, *MIT Sloan Management Review,* winter, 49, 2, 27–35

Connect using the third lens
Avoid the trap of myopia

07

> *The biggest threats are the ones you don't see coming.* **ANON**

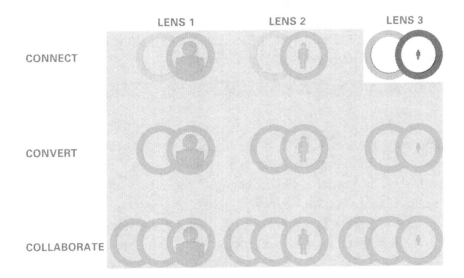

CASE STUDY

Ever tried to book a room in Milan during the yearly Salone furniture fair? Unless you want to pay triple the normal rate and book six months in advance, it is mission impossible. Hotel capacity simply cannot handle the large number of visitors to the city during that week and rates go skyrocketing because of the supply shortage. But what if you could temporarily supplement the hotel capacity in the city by using empty rooms in houses and apartments?

That was the insight Nathan Blecharczyk, Brian Chesky and Joe Gebbia had when they thought they could make some money by housing attendees at an industrial design conference on air-beds in their apartment. In 2008 they launched the website that creates the platform to connect people with space and those looking for a place to stay. Last year guest nights booked fell in the range of 12 to 15 million. On New Year's Eve alone, 141,000 people worldwide stayed at an Airbnb. The company is currently valued at $2.5 billion.

Airbnb is part of a bigger phenomenon, called the sharing economy. All around the world, people are renting out access to their house, their car, their driveway, their bicycle, their time and so on. Asset owners use digital clearing houses to capitalize on the unused capacity of things they already have, and consumers rent from their peers rather than rent or buy from a company.[1] From a fringe phenomenon, the 'sharing economy' has grown to $3.5 billion in revenue. Airbnb challenges the existing business model of the hotel industry. As it continues to grow, it represents a potentially disruptive force. Will Airbnb have the same effect on the travel industry as YouTube had on TV and bloggers have on mainstream media? Hard to predict. But certainly it's better to keep close tabs on the phenomenon than to bury your head in the sand.

B usiness history is littered with stories of companies that failed to see the destructive waves that were heading their direction, and when they finally saw the magnitude of change affecting them it was too late to respond effectively. Nevertheless, if there's one thing we know for sure, it is that change is the only constant. The average survival time of a Fortune 500 company is just 40 years. Of the companies that were on the Fortune 500 list in 1995, less than half still remain, and annual turnover has risen over the last decades.[2]

If you take a microscope to observe the ecosystem of an ant's nest you will learn a lot about the way they move and organize themselves. If you zoom in really close, you will detect there is a clear pattern in the seemingly random way they move around.[3] But you will fail to see the elephant heading in the direction of the nest, ready to trample it. The closer the look, the more we lose sight of what's in the broader picture.

To be able to see ahead, we need to adopt a wider lens. The close-up lens that we discussed in the Introduction allows us to zoom in and connect more strongly with our current customer base. The risk of using this lens exclusively is that we fail to see what is going on around us. For that, we need to use a wide lens. The wide lens gives a less detailed image of what is right in front of us, but it gives us the broadest view of what is in our peripheral vision.

When used in a business context, the term 'peripheral vision' means the ability of companies to detect, interpret and act on distant signals.[4] It's a capability that most managers admit to be lacking in their organization.[5] A shortcoming of most business analysis is that it tends to focus on the business that is right in front of us. This narrow focus on the immediate environment is necessary but not sufficient to deal with an ever-changing environment. The peripheral vision we develop by adopting a wide lens allows us to see beyond the regular offering for our usual customers. This wider lens allows us to pick up the emerging signals of:

- shifting customer needs;
- new customer segments that are emerging;
- changes in the environment that may affect the future of our business;
- new competitors that will present direct or indirect competition in the future.

To pick up these emerging signals, we do not need a crystal ball. The future is most often already present, it is just unevenly distributed. So we do not need to invent the future but we do need to be able to pick up the current signals of what is ahead. Everything that is new starts small and takes time to grow. Sudden tsunamis often only feel that way because the phenomenon was not on your radar screen until it reached significant size. We can be better prepared by picking up the signals of change before they've become too big to ignore. Take the major innovations of the past decades as an example. None of them suddenly hit the market, although we can now no longer imagine the world without refrigerators, mobile phones, computers, dishwashers, and so on. Nevertheless it took quite some time for any of these products to grow to a considerable size. Research shows that it takes anywhere between six and nine years to reach the take-off point for a new product category, ie when sales start to accelerate but are still far from the maximum. It is the point when the S-shaped growth curve that typically characterizes new product sales over time hits its inflection point. This take-off happens at an average penetration rate of just 1.7 per cent.[6] This means that it would take a hard-core optimist to consider some of the most significant innovations of the last century a success if you measured their success only two to three years after commercialization.

CASE STUDY

This is what the story of Nespresso, the illustrious business unit of Nestlé, illustrates. When you ask people when Nespresso started, many will tell you that it started about a decade ago. Not many people will be able to tell you that Nespresso started in 1986. The success was not an immediate smash hit. It took 25 years to build the brand to its current €3 billion size. If we had made the evaluation of Nespresso after two years (which in most companies represents a decent mid-term horizon where one expects to see results from a new initiative) we would probably not have bet a lot of money on its future. Very little factual evidence would have given you confidence that this new Nestlé venture would grow to its current size. Sales and profits fell well below the pre-launch forecasts and expectations. It took till 1995, nine years after its launch, for Nespresso to reach break-even.

In those early years, some of the staunchest critics of Nespresso were within the organization itself. Nestlé executives doubted whether there was any point in keeping on investing in the fledgling business unit. They wondered why it was necessary to introduce self-cannibalization to its coffee products sold in supermarkets. They questioned if Nespresso would not be more successful if it stuck closer to the traditional Nestlé business model. Nespresso had a hard time establishing credibility inside the broader organization and it only survived thanks to CEO Peter Brabeck, who shielded Nespresso from the criticism and kept on protecting it. Imagine now, knowing all this, how competitors looked at this new challenger. If not even a Nestlé executive would have vouched for its continuity, what is the likelihood that outside competitors would have believed in what was to become a formidable competitor?

The same is true for the emergence of new business models. With the luxury of hindsight, it's not difficult to predict the future. But what the story of Nespresso illustrates is that the key is to recognize the signals of change when they are still small. It is easy to spot the big evolutions in your market once they reach considerable size and feature on your radar screen. But those evolutions were already present long before, just at a much smaller scale. It is then that we need to pick them up, so that we can react early enough. That means that if you want to understand the future you can look at what's happening right now, but you have to be willing and able to pick up the weak signals. You have to be able to see the small-scale phenomena that may grow into large-scale shifts.

To allow us to do this, we need a wider lens, one that zooms out from our current customers, competitors and markets, and enables us to see the bigger picture. You may think that you already invest quite a bit in understanding the environment, analysing the research and detecting new trends. But be careful that the type of information you look at does not contain serious blind spots. Major disruptive changes often originate from the fringes of the industry. The early signals of change are therefore often not present in the standard industry reports and data sources that many companies rely on to get input about their market. This causes a problem of selective perception – burying your head in the sand and claiming you do not see any dangers on the horizon.

For example, if one wants to get a sense of the number of consumers interested in buying organic food products, one could opt to look at the current sales in supermarkets of those organic items. The conclusion would be that it is a small-scale fringe phenomenon, and that most consumers, when given the choice, prefer regular items over the organic alternatives presented to them. Standard Nielsen data on consumer food purchases would allow you to track whether there was any growth in the segment, and you would conclude it's definitely no more than a niche market. But would these standard reports ever indicate that there was a future for a company like Whole Foods Market, which built an $11 billion business on a health food proposition? By the time the company is big enough to show up on the radar screen of the biggest competitors, it has already claimed the market.

Don't get blindsided by the information sources you use. Established industry observers and data providers begin to report on a phenomenon and include it in their default view on the market when it's big enough to pay attention to. Before something becomes part of standard industry reports, it needs to have come up on the radar screen of those compiling these reports. Smart competitors take advantage of this and attack in the area of least resistance, which is also the area of least attention.

The customer trap: learn from the customers you don't have

The first area where we need to deploy a wide lens is the customers we investigate. Most organizations tend to focus on their core customer segment and their most important customers. The mantra of customer-centricity requires that you listen to your customers, but this can be very dangerous when interpreted too narrowly. In fact, being too focused on current customers is cited as a major reason why incumbents fail.[7] The work of Clayton Christensen, elected as the most influential management guru in the world, can be read as a warning against being customer-oriented.[8]

The core premise is that listening too carefully to current customers leads companies to put aside potentially disruptive innovations in favour of incremental improvements on performance dimensions that current customers appreciate. This can be extremely dangerous when disruptive forces manifest themselves, often exploited by newcomers who take advantage of incumbents' blind spots.

CASE STUDY

For example, would a Lufthansa frequent traveller, the type of person who occupies the airline's business class seats, ever point his or her airline of choice towards a low-cost airline's value proposition? More likely, he or she will ask for even better service, even more flexibility, ever more in-flight comfort and so on. Nevertheless, there was definitely an opportunity to satisfy other types of customers with a bare-bones service, as the success of low-cost airlines such as Ryanair illustrates. For incumbent airlines, the frequent business traveller is the most important segment. For example, at Virgin Airlines, this 1 per cent of customers accounts for 11 per cent of profits.[9] So it's not surprising that it also dominates their agenda when it comes to deciding which customers are the most important to satisfy. The risk is that this singular attention to high-value demanding customers leads to ignoring other potentially lucrative segments. Innovations often address new customer segments. Listening to your current customer base thus will naturally lead you in the opposite direction, missing out on major market opportunities. Low-cost airlines have found a formula to serve those customers that traditionally were neglected by airlines: the leisure customers who only fly once in a while. The results are clear. While traditional airlines scramble for profitability as they fight for the same segment of customers, low-cost airlines are the winners in the industry. For example, low-cost airline Ryanair boasts 12.5 per cent profitability, while UK rival British Airways is confronting losses.

A second danger from listening to a limited set of customers is that product development is driven more and more by a small set of customers that have specialized needs but that are not representative of the bulk of the market. Companies may work with a narrow group of customers called 'lead users' – customers who have an advanced understanding of a product and are experts in its use. Lead users can offer product ideas, but since they are not average users, the products that spring from their recommendations may have limited mass appeal.

Companies should take off the blinkers that keep them from seeing beyond their current customers.[10] The truth about whether being customer-oriented leads to undesired results thus depends on the definition of 'customer orientation'. When customer orientation is understood as listening to your best customers, this is consistent with the observation that this will not help a company deal with disruptive innovation. A customer will not lead its supplier to products that it cannot immediately utilize. Since disruptive innovations are not targeted at mainstream customers but at developing new market segments, they are not the direction in which mainstream customers will drive the industry. When customer orientation is understood as discovering the latent needs of the overall market, which includes existing, new and emerging segments, then it is not in contradiction with exploiting disruptive innovation.

The competitor trap

How to deal with the intense competitive pressure that is omnipresent in just about any market? The tendency is to get wrapped up in destructive competitive battles in an attempt to preserve market share or market dominance. In spite of being the potential way out, we see that firms operating in a highly competitive environment are actually less likely to be strategically innovative.[11] It is a natural reaction for firms that are faced with strong competition to focus all their energy and resources on dealing with these competitive battles. Unfortunately, that leaves little time and scant energy and resources to take a step back and consider alternative paths. It is precisely those firms who need to adopt the wide lens the most, that least consider the possibilities it offers! When the direct competitive battles heat up, opening up the scope of opportunities matters the most. Scanning for alternative strategic directions provides a way for firms to turn around the negative effect of a highly competitive environment, enabling them to escape the battle for supremacy by choosing to occupy a position in which they can escape cutthroat direct competition.

When directing competitive intelligence efforts, companies tend to look at a limited number of competitors. It has been shown that companies see a remarkably small set of companies as their competitors. Even in situations when the set of competitors is quite large, there are on average only six to nine companies that are really considered to be part of the 'competitive set'.[12] This competitive set are those companies that decision makers consider to be their focal competitors. It represents their mental model of the competitive landscape.

CASE STUDY

For example, a telecom company I worked with had set up a taskforce for competitive intelligence, to collect, analyse and disseminate information on competitors' actions and decisions. To guide this mission, the taskforce identified a set of 10 competitors that they considered as core. Given the usual six to nine competitors, this was an exceptionally extensive exercise. Each of these competitors was vetted, and the taskforce did a great job making sure that none of the relevant information on any of the 10 went unnoticed. Colleagues received regular updates with the headlines. An online knowledge centre was set up to be an easily accessible information source for anybody who needed it.

Three years later the company started to lose market share. Upon further investigation, it turned out that its biggest threat had not come from any of the 10 focal competitors that had received all of its attention. It had actually been a newcomer with an alternative technology. The company was completely blindsided.

Who should you consider as you competitor? It is clear that companies do not regard their competitive landscape as a homogeneous group. Some competitors are considered 'focal': immediate threats. Others are considered less relevant. The classification of firms as focal competitors is based on a continuum on a number of attributes, based on similarity or size.[13] What this means is that the companies we mostly consider to be our competitors are those that are either the biggest players in our industry, or the ones that are most like us. Smaller competitors or competitors who are different from us are less likely to be considered 'focal'. They are not seen as direct threats. The competitive set is thus populated by the market leader and all the companies most similar to us in terms of size, strategy, locations, etc.

There is nothing immediately wrong with this as such. It helps us navigate a complex landscape, simplify and speed up decision making and make competitive intelligence a feasible task. But, it also leads to a rather myopic view that can be dangerous when threats emerge from outside of immediate view. By defining a focal set of competitors, we bias the competitive analysis towards a very small set of competitors that is not representative of the full arena. This means that interpretation of competitive actions is affected by our own mental model of the competition;[14] this mental model is developed mainly by examining our biggest and most similar competitors.[15]

The impact of the competitive set can be seen at three different levels. First, competitors inside the competitive set receive the most attention. The competitive set thus works as an information filter. But the recognition of competitors as similar counterparts not only increases attention to their actions, it also lends relevance to them. This means that actions from competitors inside of the competitive set are seen as having the highest impact on our own competitive position. Finally, actions from competitors within the competitive set are also given more credibility. This means that their actions are seen as smarter and more successful than if those same actions came from a competitor from outside the competitive set.

All of this means that if we have a rigorous competitive intelligence process, we may have the illusion of an objective view on the competitive landscape. But the truth is that this is just a smoke screen for a heavily skewed view on reality. As we pay more attention, relevance and credibility to whatever companies inside the competitive set do, the opposite holds true for companies outside of the competitive set. Automatically we pay less attention to them, we feel what they're doing is not relevant for us, and we don't attach any credibility to them. In other words, we completely underestimate the actions coming from outside the competitive set. This explains how a simple low-end product from a small company could invade the digital camera market that was populated by the consumer electronics giants.

How was it possible that consumer electronics giants like Sony and Kodak were blindsided by the Flip? Two explanations clarify why this can happen. First, Pure Digital did not belong to the focal competitive set of the incumbents in the camcorder market; it was a total newcomer. Secondly, Pure Digital did not focus on the same product

CASE STUDY

When Pure Digital Technologies introduced its Flip point-and-shoot camcorder in 2007, it dramatically simplified video recording. The device, measuring just a little bigger than a deck of cards, was designed to provide an easy and simple way to make video and upload it to the internet, especially to popular sharing sites like YouTube. The Flip cost less than $150 and its videos could be e-mailed in one quick process. The innovative built-in USB connector made sure no cables were needed to upload and share video or to charge the device. Pure Digital created a camera that even the famous critic Walt Mossberg from the *Wall Street Journal* approved of.[16]

There was however one feature the Flip missed compared to competitors: 1080p high definition recording. Just two years after its introduction, Cisco bought Pure Digital for $590 million. At that time it was the best-selling camcorder on Amazon. It was also only then that the success of Pure Digital's original Flip attracted a slew of copycat products. That did not daunt Pure Digital however. Its CEO Jonathan Kaplan was quoted saying: 'Imitation is an absolutely fine form of flattery. I'm happy every time a competitor launches a new product.' Indeed the Flip continued to rise to an astonishing 35 per cent of the camcorder market.[17]

features as the incumbents. Instead of competing on image quality, Pure Digital competed on price, ease-of-use and share-ability. In fact, it was a conscious decision not to include the highest resolution so the Flip could be sold at very competitive prices. However, from the viewpoint of existing competitors, that made the Flip an inferior camera. Not surprisingly, they therefore did not react right away, giving Pure Digital free rein to grow in the market.

On blinkers and biases

The third lens takes us the furthest from day-to-day business. It's where we pay attention to the periphery of the market: away from existing customers, away from existing products and further into the future. That means we get further away from familiar territory, and interpreting signals becomes harder. The potential for misinterpretation is great. When scanning for signals of emerging change, the difficulty is not so much in finding information: it is in deciding what to attend to and what you can ignore. Interpretation is thus the hardest task, a task which is loaded with potential pitfalls.

The biggest pitfall comes from our own blinkers and biases. There are a number of booby traps to avoid when deploying the third lens. The first trap is the type of signals you search for and pay attention to. What enters your radar screen?

Attention traps

Using a wide lens to scan the environment creates an instant and uncontrollable wealth of information signals that might be appropriate for the decision at hand, or irrelevant. Managers need to structure all possible information signals to capture the essence. When should we interpret a signal as significant and when can we ignore it?

We earlier referred to the danger of focusing too much on current competitors or customers, leading to a customer trap and a competitor trap. Indeed, what we pay attention to is what we take action on.[18] Failure to pay attention to the periphery of the market implies that we will be slow in responding to it. Using the wide lens implies that we zoom away from the status quo.

CASE STUDY

In a variant on a classic experiment, I often present my MBA students with the following test. I show them a deck of cards, and draw one card after another from the stack. Some cards I keep, some I toss away.
I challenge them to find out the rule behind the decision to toss or keep a card, and to only state it when they're absolutely sure. The actual decision rule that I use is one where I keep alternating colours. However, I've deliberately arranged the cards up front such that they appear in increasing order, and showing a

pattern of even or uneven numbers. Invariably, after a few cards one student will blurt out that he found the answer: that I only keep the even number. When I probe for the thinking process behind the answer, it goes something like this. After a few draws, the student formulates an initial hypothesis (eg only the even numbers are kept). When one or two subsequent draws confirm that hypothesis, the conclusion is final. Instead of formulating an alternative hypothesis and observing whether this would also fit, we tend to look only for confirmation of what we already believe. This is called 'confirmation bias'.

When scanning the environment, confirmation bias is a dangerous thing, because it means that we only pay attention to the signals that confirm what we already believe and ignore the others. This selective perception effect means that we impose our own frame of reference in selecting the type of information we pay attention to.

People have a strong tendency to rationalize away any new information that does not confirm their preconceived notions. This tendency to ignore information that does not confirm our beliefs is the driving force behind a stubborn commitment to the wrong path. Even if new information appears that tells us this is the wrong path, we fail to incorporate it into our judgement and just follow the same course.[19]

Interpretation traps

It is one thing to identify relevant signals, but we also need to be able to make sense of them. How do we interpret the magnitude of impact of what's happening outside and how do we decide on the right way forward? Interpretation doesn't come without its difficulties.

For one thing, it is human nature to favour the status quo: we use the current situation as the reference point for comparing the alternative. This ignores the fact that the status quo is probably not going to remain the status quo, and will be subject to change anyhow. We should complement the question 'What if we do…?' with 'What if we don't…?' The projected value of a decision must be assessed against a range of scenarios, the most realistic of which is often a deteriorating competitive and financial future.[20] For example, when making a decision on whether to launch a new product or not we should ask ourselves not only, 'How much more are we going to sell if we do?' but also, 'How much less are we going to sell if we don't?' This creates a completely different business case.

The biggest enemies of unbiased analysis are the ideas that are already in our head. When making decisions or talking to others, people use mental models of the world to evaluate choices and frame discussions. A mental model is a simplified view of how things work, which allows you to cut through the complexity and deal with information overload. Managers have a mental model of the business they operate in. This mental model contains all your beliefs about what it entails to do business in an industry. It is something that you build up over time through experience. Statements reflective of your mental model are, for example: 'Our products cannot be sold online', 'Our mark-up should be at least 150 per cent', 'You need to be a trained engineer to sell our complicated solutions', 'Bypassing the distributor will immediately lead to repercussions', 'You need your own R&D department to remain competitive', or 'An online MBA degree will never have the credibility of a traditional one.' These are examples of what we define as the 'dominant logic'. The dominant logic is present in the deeply held assumptions that govern your business. They are the conventions nobody questions. It is a mindset, worldview or conceptualization of the business and what is required to operate in it successfully. The dominant logic can exist at the level of individual firms, but also at the level of an entire industry. Industry members share similar experiences and similar environments, and therefore also share similar mental models.

These default mental models are mental traps. They lead to a phenomenon called 'cramming': all new information is interpreted in such a way that it fits the existing mental model. Change only happens at the point when new information is so profoundly at odds with our long-held assumptions that it impels a change in the belief structure.

One company I worked with deliberately challenged these assumptions by studying how other industries operate. They then asked themselves the 'What if' question: 'What if this practice would work in our industry?' It's an exercise in mental flexibility to challenge one's own thinking and to dare to think through, at least hypothetically, what would be the alternatives if your never-questioned industry rules turned out to be not true.

Threat versus opportunity?

Beauty is in the eye of the beholder. The same phenomenon may be judged very differently depending on who makes the judgement and the same evolution could be seen as a threat or an opportunity. Threats are defined as situations in which loss is a likely outcome, and over which one has relatively little control. Opportunities are situations in which gain is a likely outcome, and over which one has at least a reasonable degree of control. Is the tablet phenomenon an opportunity for magazine publishers because it allows them to enrich their content with new features and make it available in a different format to their readers, or is it a threat because tablet users might be less inclined to buy a magazine as they have already a wealth of online content at their fingertips? Whether you see it as a threat or an opportunity will have a great impact on how you respond to it.[21]

Seeing a new phenomenon as a threat leads to a bigger commitment and more resource spend. That is why change consultants prompt you to 'create a sense of urgency' by highlighting the bad news. However, seeing a new phenomenon as a threat also makes you retreat

CASE STUDY

This was imminently clear in the contrasting views that Charles Schwab and Merrill Lynch had on online stock trading. The former called 'investment, along with e-mail and pornography, one of the "natural" uses of the internet'. The latter framed it 'a serious threat to Americans' financial lives'. Guess who ploughed in first? Charles Schwab embraced the internet and launched online trading three years ahead of Merrill Lynch.

into the trenches rather than embrace the change. Decision makers may spend more money dealing with a threat but they do so defensively, and with very little intention of making big changes to their current business model. They just want to minimize the threat and avert it, and then hopefully go back to business as usual. Decision makers who frame a new phenomenon as an opportunity act very differently. They are more open to try new things.

The boiling frog syndrome

If you drop a frog in a pot of boiling water, it will frantically try to clamber out. But if you place it gently in a pot of tepid water and turn the heat on low, it will float there quite placidly. As the water gradually heats up, the frog will sink into a tranquil stupor, just like any of us in a hot bath, and before long, with a smile on its face, it will allow itself to be boiled to death.[22] The story of the boiling frog, whether true or not, serves as a warning. As we see signals of change, and downplay their long-term impact, we might get trapped in inaction while the environment is shifting.

Astonishment report

When new employees join, they can still look at the organization with a virgin eye. They are not hindered by the curse of knowledge and can look with a fresh perspective.

The 'astonishment report' tries to capture that fresh perspective. It is a report that new employees are asked to write after just a few months within the organization. It describes what surprises them, what they find odd and what was unexpected. It is a reflection on the things they would approach differently.

Are you ready to have a mirror held up to you?

There is a clear recipe for avoiding the many blinkers and biases that affect our judgement in interpreting new signals. The basis of our problem in judging accurately is the curse of knowledge and experience. The longer our experience, the more tainted our judgement. The solution is to involve a virgin eye – bring in newcomers and outsiders. Don't disqualify their judgement, but look at it as an untainted point of view.

Driving attention to the outside

As the previous section shows, we need an early warning system that allows us to scan the environment for emerging developments in terms of customer needs, market segments or competitors. By deploying a broader lens, we make sure we remove the myopic attention paid to current customers and competitors and take a broader view. While this broader view can never have the same intensity of focus that we have on our existing customer base, it allows us to see further ahead. What we need is the willingness to devote time and energy to external scanning.

There are known knowns, known unknowns and unknown unknowns. Successful scanning tackles all three by using passive information absorption, active information hunting, targeted probing and broad-based explorations.

Active and passive scanning

The goal of scanning is to pick up the weak signals before they manifest themselves on a larger scale. This can happen passively. Every day there are people within the company who hear and see things – sales people on the road, R&D people at a conference, administrators in an industry organization meeting and so on. Unwittingly, they pick up a lot of information. To make that disparate information useful we need to bring it together and detect the systemic patterns that manifest themselves. Active scanning happens when we set up a search for information, either directed by concrete questions and hypotheses, or explorative.

Learn beyond the usual suspects

Developing our peripheral vision means going beyond the usual suspects, learning from the customers we don't have and the competitors we don't (yet) have. Do you do the post-mortem analysis of lost contracts to find out why you lost out? Do you talk to users who do not use your product? Do you select non-customers as participants for market research? Do you analyse what are the substitute products and why some customers prefer them over yours? Do you find out where churned customers went? Do you ask yourself what the blind spots are, not covered by your regular industry reports?

Train your muscles

Concrete exercises can help to direct attention to the outside. Scenario analysis aims at imagining the different shapes the future could take, and how to tackle that. War-room exercises can be used to put yourself in a competitor's shoes and ask what the most likely next moves from their point of view would be.

Reverse mentoring

Follow in the footsteps of companies like Cisco, Ogilvy & Mather and GE.

In an effort to school senior executives in technology, social media and the latest workplace trends, many businesses are pairing upper management with younger employees. The senior execs stay up to date on how the younger generation uses communication technology. At the same time, they feel the pulse of younger recruits within the organization. The junior mentors gain access to a senior exec level where they rarely get heard.

The benefits? Better workplace relationships, no different speeds in adopting new technology, and employee satisfaction.

How to exploit the wide lens

Using the wide lens effectively is not an easy task. On the one hand, there is the challenge of overlooking important emerging phenomena;

on the other there is the challenge of being overcome by the multitude of small signals to pay attention to.

Take, for example, the emergence of Google Glass. The fledgling new technology is currently being tested by a number of carefully selected geeks and technology-enthusiasts, under wide media attention. Should we go ahead and develop a strategy for Google Glass? Hard to say. The jury is still out on whether Google Glass will be a gadget only for nerds and geeks, or the beginning of a revolution where all of us will wear a tiny screen on our face.

There are two different ways to deal with this challenge.[23] The first is to adopt a wait-and-see attitude, only responding to signals when they reach a certain magnitude and certitude. You can bet that Google Glass will take a long time to catch on and that there will be a lot of different versions before the ultimate application is found. You can decide only to step in when it is clear which direction it is going. The risk of this strategy is to be one step behind, which may make it difficult to catch up.

The second strategy is to lead the pack and give full commitment to a course of action. That is to start preparing an application to give your company a presence in the new technology. The risk of this strategy is to commit too soon and waste resources.

There is, however, a third way, which is to probe and learn, dipping your toe in the water to feel the temperature, and diving in only when you're sure it's right. Within this strategy, the goal is to develop a series of small-scale experiments, trying different things with the intention of learning as much as possible. This is better because:

- Learning through action is more effective than learning through observation. Although there is a great deal that you can learn from watching others, there are always lessons that you can only learn from getting involved yourself.

- Setting up small-scale actions allows you to start developing new skills, and gives you a head start for later larger-scale investments.

- It creates a culture of learning within the organization.

The wall of shame

The wall of shame serves the same purpose as a wall of fame: to make a showcase in a public spot with a lot of passers-by. But it shows the failures of the company: the products that did not work, the projects that were killed, the early attempts of the company's current products, etc.

The wall of shame is a way to celebrate failure, and not hide the projects and initiatives that were not successful. By showing them we demonstrate there is no shame attached to failure, there is only shame attached to a lack of trying. The wall of shame shows that success was inevitably preceded by failed attempts. It illustrates the saying: success is 99 per cent failure.

When should you use any of these three ways to deal with emerging change? Figure 7.1 depicts the four different routes to deploy the wide lens. The framework is based on two different dimensions describing the change context you are confronted with. The first dimension addresses the rate of change on the environment: are you in a dynamic or undynamic situation? The second dimension considers how far from the core business the emerging change is taking you.

- *Undynamic and known*: in an environment with a slow pace of change, where the change is occurring in familiar territory, you can hold onto the current strategy. Just be vigilant enough to not fall asleep: stable waters can quickly turn into a violent storm.

- *Dynamic and known*: in a fast-changing environment, where the extent of change is in familiar territory, you need to embrace continuous adaptation. This is a situation where you need to constantly adapt to new signals, and where the organization is in a permanent state of flux without much rest.

- *Undynamic and unknown*: in a slow-changing environment, where change is forcing you to envision unknown territory, you need to prepare yourself by adopting strong peripheral vision. Keeping a close eye on the evolutions in the market, you react when the time is right. The biggest risk in this situation is

FIGURE 7.1 Change dimensions

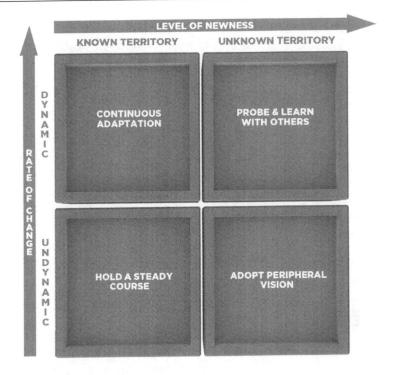

The post-mortem analysis

Jonathan Rosenberg, Senior Vice President of Products at Google, asks each of his teams to do a post-mortem analysis of a failure and publish it for everybody else.

Mistakes should not be buried or hidden. There are more learning opportunities in mistakes than in successes. But the learning only happens if we are willing to take a closer look, understand exactly what went wrong, so we can prevent this from happening in the future.

to underestimate the rate of change in your environment and be surprised when the pace accelerates.

- *Dynamic and unknown:* the more you are in unknown territory, the more learning is required and the more important a probe and learn strategy. Many small initiatives can help to explore opportunities while minimizing risk. You need to create actions where risk is minimized and learning is maximized. The risk can be further minimized by sharing it with others. This is the situation we explore in the next chapters.

In short

- Using the third lens means doing a constant wide scan of the market and the environment to detect new evolutions and emerging trends. With this, we zoom out from current customers, competitors and markets to see the bigger picture.

- We need to avoid the customer trap and the competitors trap. That means learning from the customers we currently do not have, and focusing on the competitors that are newly emerging and not part of the standard competitive set.

- The challenge of interpretation is the biggest when we use the third lens, as we get further away from familiar territory and have less in-depth knowledge to tap into. It is especially challenging to make sure interpretation of signals is not fraught with blinkers and biases.

- When we turn our attention outside, we need to do this with a virgin eye, not hindered by the legacy of past experiences and past mental models.

- The best way to predict the future is to participate in it. And the future is already here, just unevenly distributed. In a dynamic and unknown environment, a probe and learn strategy offers the best opportunity to maximize learning.

Get started

- Allocate resources (time and people) to competitive intelligence.

- Investigate competitors beyond the usual suspects.

- Don't underestimate small-scale phenomena: they may be the signals of emerging change.

- Make a regular agenda point of including discussions on wide lens analysis.

- Become aware of your own biases. Bring in outsiders who can introduce a fresh, unbiased perspective.

- Whenever possible, replace passive outside observation with action-based learning from practice.

Notes

1 Airbnb and the unstoppable rise of the sharing economy, *Forbes*, 23 January 2013

2 Stangler, D and Arbesman, S (2012) *What does Fortune 500 Turnover mean?* Ewing Marion Kauffman Foundation, June

3 For those really interested in movement in ant's nests, take a look at Deborah Gordon's TED talk on the subject: http://www.ted.com/talks/deborah_gordon_digs_ants.html

4 Day, G and Schoemaker, P (2006) *Peripheral Vision*, Harvard Business Review Press, Boston, MA

5 Day, G *et al* (2010) The vigilant organization, *Rotman Magazine*, autumn

6 Golder, P and Tellis, G (1997) Will it ever fly? *Marketing Science*, 16, 3, 97–127

7 Christensen, C (1997) *The Innovator's Dilemma*, Harvard Business Review Press, Boston, MA

8 http://hbr.org/web/slideshows/the-50-most-influential-management-gurus/1-christensen

9 http://www.nytimes.com/2013/09/08/business/at-virgin-america-a-fine-line-between-pizazz-and-profit.html?pagewanted=4&_r=0

10 Gilbert, C (2003) The disruption opportunity, *MIT Sloan Management Review*, summer, 27–32

11 Debruyne, M and Schoovaert, M (2006) *Innovation Outside the Lab*, FDC Knowledge Center

12 Clark, B H and Montgomery, D B (1999) Managerial identification of competitors, *Journal of Marketing*, 63, July, 67–83

13 Clark, B H and Montgomery, D B (1999) Managerial identification of competitors, *Journal of Marketing*, 63, July, 67–83

14 Kaplan, S (2011) Research in cognition and strategy: Reflections on two decades of progress and a look to the future, *Journal of Management Studies*, 48, 3, 665–95

15 Haveman, H A (1993) Follow the leader: mimetic isomorphism and entry into new markets, *Administrative Science Quarterly*, 38, 593–627

16 The Mossberg Solution, *Wall Street Journal*, 4 June 2008

17 The story of the Flip ends on a sour note though. In 2009, Cisco decided to refocus on its core business. That meant less attention on the consumer products division that it had started to build. Pure Digital was the casualty of this decision. It was closed down in 2009.

18 Ocasio, W (1997) Towards an attention-based view of the firm, *Strategic Management Journal*, 18, 187–206

19 Biyalogorsky, E *et al* (2006) Stuck in the past. Why managers persist with new product failures, *Journal of Marketing*, 70, 108–21

20 Christensen, C *et al* (2008) Innovation killers, *Harvard Business Review*, January

21 Gilbert, C (2006) Change in the presence of residual fit: Can competing frames coexist? *Organization Science*, 17, 1, 150–67

22 http://en.wikipedia.org/wiki/Boiling_frog

23 Day, G and Schoemaker, P (2006) *Peripheral Vision*, Harvard Business Review Press, Boston, MA

Convert the third lens in business model renewal

08

> *I know that we will make mistakes along the way – some will be self-inflicted, some will be served up by smart and hard-working competitors. Our passion for pioneering will drive us to explore narrow passages, and, unavoidably, many will turn out to be blind alleys. But – with a bit of good fortune – there will also be a few that open up into broad avenues.* **JEFF BEZOS, 2012**

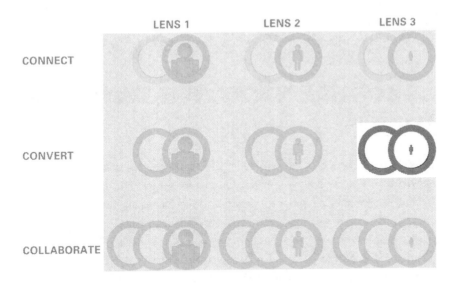

Many industries are confronted with sweeping changes. Publishing, media, pharmaceuticals, gaming, retailing, entertainment, software… all are confronted with emerging change and new business models. It's happening for the fast-moving consumer goods companies that battle the increasing dominance of private labels. It's happening for the bricks and mortar retailers that wonder what their place will be in an e-commerce world. It's happening for the pharma companies that see their R&D-dominant model crumbling. It's happening for media companies that can no longer make money from content and find advertising revenues under pressure. It's happening for hardware companies that see commoditization happening faster and faster. All of these are changes that require them to rethink their business model – changes that slowly but surely creep up on established players as their existing business models become redundant.

Earlier we introduced the concept of the wide lens. The wide lens allows us to pick up the emerging signals of change in our environment, whether introduced by shifting customer needs, new market segments, new conditions in the external environment or new competitors. These broader shifts also force us to rethink our business model for the market. When we focus on customer needs, the business model needs to follow. This requires willingness and flexibility to change the business model when the opportunity presents itself.

CASE STUDY

Consider the story of how the milk industry has gone sour. In spite of heavily sponsored awareness campaigns, demand for milk has been in free fall in developed countries for decades. US milk consumption has dropped 36 per cent since the 1970s. The dairy industry's plight is a cautionary tale for other industries whose core product falls out of favour. It illustrates the dangers of focusing on just one highly commoditized product, ignoring market trends, and trying valiantly to sell what you make rather than to make what people want.

The milk industry has nobody to blame but itself. It's in trouble because it has focused on cows instead of consumers.[1] Its focus has been largely on operational efficiency: from milking efficiency through automated machines at the farm, through economies of scale and generating supply chain efficiencies. While it has succeeded in gaining those efficiencies, they went hand-in-hand with a decline in demand. Meanwhile, others have captured great returns from the popularity of milk-based products or milk alternatives. Milk producers have not been active participants in the booming market of plant-based milk such as soya and almond milk. They have not reaped the rewards from the growth in milk-based coffee products (ie your Starbucks drink is likely to contain more milk than coffee). And they have not experienced any of the success of the Greek yoghurt phenomenon, exemplified by brands like Chobani. The company's now famous Greek yogurt is netting more than $1 billion in annual sales – and it only went to market in 2005.[2] Meanwhile traditional milk producers still push cumbersome gallon-sized cartons in inconvenient packages on the market. By pouring money into 'Drink more milk' campaigns they still hope to resurrect consumers' interest in pouring themselves a glass of milk.

Milk producers clearly defined themselves from a product perspective, not a consumer perspective. In spite of the decrease in milk consumption, the consumption of dairy-based drinks and nutritional products has been rising steadily. Of course, to reap the rewards of this rising market would require a fundamental shift in the milk production and distribution model.

Had the milk producers applied customer-focused thinking, they would have seen there was an opportunity to add value for customers by extending the value chain towards milk-based products. They also would have recognized that they needed to fundamentally rethink their production-based business model.

In this chapter, we discuss how a firm can go about making itself ready to tackle fundamental shifts in its business model. How do we implement the business model innovation that is sparked by changing customer needs or brought forward by uncharted market opportunities?

Business model innovation: fad or fab?

A lot has been said and written about business model innovation in the last decade. And a lot of that has been driven by the eye-catching performance of some great companies such as Apple, Amazon, Netflix, easyJet and Salesforce.com.

The common thread running through all these success stories is that the companies in question did not innovate in the traditional sense by investing in R&D and then launching next-generation products, but instead challenged conventional thinking within their industry. They reshaped the way business is done, all the while focusing firmly on delivering customer value to their target customer. This entailed rethinking their target markets, customer needs and wants, and the entire value delivery process. Apple, for example, focused on consumers more than business users. It emphasized usability, design and convenience over pure technological performance. And it bundled hardware, software and content in a revised ecosystem.

These examples have inspired many established companies to follow the lead of these newcomers and to think about business model innovation. They organize business model innovation workshops and start integrating business model tools and frameworks, such as the business model canvas,[3] in their standard documents and plans. They even, like Siemens has done, set up internal business model innovation consulting units.

In spite of these efforts, there has been limited impact on the actual business. Many companies are disillusioned about their attempts at business model innovation, which often remain more creative exercises than real market activity. And they fail to integrate the idea of business model innovation within their core business, seeing it as a fringe activity.

When done well, business model innovation holds the promise of many benefits. It is indeed the case that companies that innovate from the business model do better than those that only innovate from the product or service. There are three reasons for this:

1 *They are unique.* Companies that innovate the business model occupy a unique position in the competitive landscape. They avoid head-to-head competition. Coupled with this are the advantages of uniqueness: a first-mover advantage, a (temporary) monopoly, switching costs and subsequent customer loyalty. Strategic innovators also develop resources and unique capabilities. They employ different resources and often attract different customer segments than traditional competitors. Accordingly, they experience less competition for resources on both the input and output sides.

2 *They do not conform.* Business model innovators do not follow the norms of the industry. They break with the existing dominant logic of 'this is how we do things, and this is what it takes to be successful'. It's therefore difficult to pigeonhole business model innovators, and as such nobody sees them as competitors right away. They can fly below the radar much longer than competitors that go for the direct attack.

3 *They cannot be copied.* One of the reasons firms enjoy superior performance through business model innovation is that they erect imitation barriers. Companies that have been successful strategic innovators have often developed a set of unique skills to operate their business model. This makes it very difficult to copy: an imitator would have to replicate the new skills underlying it, turning its whole organization upside down. This lack of imitation reinforces the performance of strategic innovators and enables them to establish first-mover advantages in building up a unique position in the industry.

In light of these benefits, why do companies fail with business model innovation? It's not usually for lack of ideas – coming up with ideas is the easy part. Two culprits are more to blame: a failure to work outside-in and a failure to execute.

An important reason for the lacklustre track record of business model innovation inside established companies is that we have lost track of the reason for investing in business model innovation. We forget to work outside-in. Business model innovation is not an end-goal in and of itself; it is only a means to an end. That end is driven by the customer in mind. When you engage in a business model innovation initiative, the first thing to realize is that success starts by not thinking about business models at all, but thinking about the opportunity to satisfy a real customer who needs a job done. The second step is to construct a blueprint laying out how your company will fulfil that need at a profit.[4] In our enthusiasm for business model innovation, we tend to forget that the first step is actually the most important one. That's what the reverse value chain teaches us.

The second culprit is a failure to execute. Business model innovation too often remains a theoretical exercise rather than a reality. This happens because established companies often do not push forward or fail to commit resources. Why this is happening will be clarified in the next few pages.

Enemy number 1: The fear of cannibalization

Most companies die not because they do the wrong things, but because they keep doing what used to be the right things for too long. To a large extent this is sparked by the fear of cannibalization.

The biggest enemy of innovation is the unwillingness of decision makers to cannibalize their existing business.[5] The more you are successful, the more you have to lose. It is, however, exactly that fear that can lead to the company's demise. Anybody who has tried championing an innovation that could potentially pose a threat to the existing business will be able to confirm that cannibalization is the main argument you will be confronted with. Established companies differ from start-ups in one aspect: they have an existing business to consider and defend, and any new undertaking will have to fight for resources with, and be seen in light of, this established business. More often than not, this means that innovations lose out on both aspects. Either the new business is not guaranteed to deliver the same rate of return as the established business, with the same level of confidence, and/or the new business might negatively impact the established business. In both cases it makes sense to continue as before and allocate more resources to the established business instead of to the uncertain new business.

CASE STUDY

The story of Netflix serves as a clear warning against this reflex. The company has already beaten DVD rental giant Blockbuster, and has its eye now on the vastly bigger video-on-demand market. Netflix, an online subscription-based DVD rental service, was first conceived by Reed Hastings after he discovered an overdue rental copy of 'Apollo 13' in his cupboard. After paying the $40 late fee, Hastings began to consider alternative ways to provide a home movie service that would better satisfy customers.

Founded in 1999 and based in Los Gatos, California, Netflix in its original incarnation was a web-based catalogue service that rented older, lesser-known movies in DVD format and delivered the merchandise by mail. From the company's inception, CEO Reed Hastings and his management team sought to ensure that they understood which services their customers wanted. Netflix quickly realized that though customers had to wait for days to receive their DVDs, they preferred the slower pace over the hassle of choosing, renting and returning videos from conventional retailers. Thus was born Netflix's innovative subscription service, which allowed customers to keep videos for as long as they wished, offering convenience and choice.

By year-end 2003, Netflix demonstrated that a profitable business model could be built on that value proposition. With $272 million revenue, it returned a positive net income for the first time. Its 1.5 million subscribers could use Netflix's website to choose from among over 55,000 different titles. Netflix's flagship subscription plan offered unlimited monthly rentals, allowing customers to keep up to three movies in their possession at any one time for a monthly fee of $19.99. Industry incumbent Blockbuster at the same time could not turn its $5.9 billion revenue into a positive bottom line due to the heavy fixed costs of its vast retail network and DVD catalogue. Its value proposition catered to the impulse decision of going to get a movie to watch right away – Blockbuster's target was to be within 10 minutes of every person.

It was a model that was quickly losing ground. Nevertheless, Blockbuster remained oblivious to the Netflix threat, claiming:

> *Obviously, we pay attention to any way people are getting home entertainment. We always look at all those things. We have not seen a business model that's financially viable long-term in this arena. Online rental services are serving a niche market.*

Blockbuster, with more than 10 per cent of its revenues coming from late fees, obviously had a lot to lose. Three months later, clarifying that Blockbuster did not intend to launch an online business to compete with Netflix, a spokesperson announced, 'We don't believe there is enough of a demand for mail order – it's not a sustainable business model.' Not until 2003 did Blockbuster's management publicly discuss Netflix by name as a threat to its core business model and it did not formally respond to Netflix until the introduction of Blockbuster Online in 2004. Blockbuster's reaction proved to be too little, too late, as it was unable to catch up with Netflix's lead in the online DVD rental business.

During Netflix's rise, industry observers anointed video-on-demand (VoD) as the 'next big thing' in home video. Many industry observers believed that the option for customers to order movies through their computers for instant viewing would quickly impact the large user base of Netflix's core business. Those who found online DVD rentals and traditional video stores to be inconvenient would now be able to watch their selection immediately, without waiting for it to arrive via the mail or even leaving their home. Hastings recognized that reality:

> *If I survey my customers and ask, 'Do you want the low-quality internet offering being downloaded to your computer?' I'll get a response telling me that .001 per cent of customers are interested in it. So, by being customer-centric, I would probably say downloading is snake oil.*

But Hastings was planning Netflix's strategic response accordingly:

> *We are actively investing in VoD and will continue to try and find niches where downloading is actually a better solution for the customer. You know it's not going to be a mainstream customer.*[6]

That's changing. Netflix's most recent deals have moved it from the periphery of the home-entertainment ecosystem into the centre of a world in which consumers can watch films and TV shows anytime, anywhere. In the Summer of 2011, Netflix was even criticized by analysts and consumers alike for wanting to move too fast ahead, breaking its original postal mail model away from its online streaming model. Netflix's CEO explains why he was pushing forward:

For the past five years, my greatest fear at Netflix has been that we wouldn't make the leap from success in DVDs to success in streaming. Most companies that are great at something – like AOL dialup or Borders bookstores – do not become great at new things people want (streaming for us) because they are afraid to hurt their initial business. Eventually these companies realize their error of not focusing enough on the new thing, and then the company fights desperately and hopelessly to recover.[7]

Netflix's strategy is to deliver entertainment that best fits a customer's interest, time and place – it started out as DVDs by mail, switching to on-demand streaming and probably something else in the future. Netflix's latest move is to develop unique content (with the critically-acclaimed series 'House of Cards'). As Netflix CEO Reed Hastings put it: 'Companies rarely die from moving too fast, and they frequently die from moving too slowly.'[8] The result of this philosophy is a $3.67 billion revenue company with 33 million customers in 40 different countries. For one low monthly price, Netflix members can watch as much as they want, anytime, anywhere, on nearly any internet-connected screen. Additionally, in the United States subscribers can receive DVDs and Blu-ray discs delivered quickly to their homes.

The story of Netflix contains a few important insights. First, its original online DVD rental model was based on a value proposition that enhanced the customer journey where Blockbuster's model faltered. While Blockbuster brought the latest movies and was within easy reach of the customer, its model had some distinct disadvantages. It required customers to come back quickly to return the movie, or get a penalty. Netflix's model allowed customers to keep the movie indefinitely. Blockbuster did not offer customers much choice of movies, as it faced the limitations of its outlet space. Netflix offered a huge selection, helping customers navigate through it. Blockbuster did not reduce the purchase risk, as it offered little guidance on what movie to choose, while Netflix developed as one of its key resources a recommendation algorithm that guides customers easily through its vast range of movies.

A second lesson from Netflix is that the company always has its focus on the value proposition for the customer, and pushes forward to bring the best solution for customers, even if that means cannibalizing its existing business. The company operates firmly on the principle that cannibalization does not mean shooting yourself in the foot: it means shooting yourself in the foot before anybody else does. Self-cannibalization is the best remedy against competitive attacks.

Rational and irrational inertia

Why do incumbents fail when confronted with the need to transform their business model? Rationally, if an innovation represents an opportunity that yields a return greater than the cost of capital it should be attractive to invest in, whether the investor is an incumbent, new entrant or start-up.

As we described above, the fear of cannibalization is the number one enemy. But there are other obstacles to overcome. Some of these are rational reasons that lead to inertia, others are less rational. Let's first explore the irrational sources why incumbents hold off from moving forward with investing in new business models. Aside from the well-known 'not-invented-here' syndrome, status quo bias and resistance to change that almost all human beings suffer from, there are a number of barriers which are more specific to business model innovation.

Myopia

In the previous chapter, we talked about the customer trap and the competitor trap. Both lead to myopia, towards the current customers and current competitors. This myopia causes a lack of attention to what is happening in the periphery of the market, which is often where new business models arise. It is to alleviate the danger of myopia that we need to exploit the wide lens.

Stickiness of the mental model

A mental model is very sticky: you cannot get rid of it easily. For example, the dominant mental model for business schools includes beliefs about the importance of research, the value of MBA rankings, importance of in-class interaction with students, etc. Even though the success of Massive Open Online Courses (MOOCs) and online MBA programmes has shown that this mental model should be questioned, most faculty members still hold on to the old belief set. Mental models are built up over time, based on past experiences and established beliefs, and are deeply rooted within the organization. They are the lens through which we view the world. Unless we really can no longer hide from the fact that our dominant logic is wrong, we will hold onto it.

Why is it so hard to change your mental model? First, it's embedded within your whole thinking; secondly, it's not something you're actively aware of. You just use your mental model as a frame of reference, actually the only frame of reference that you know. It works as an information filter and it influences the way you interpret information: anything that fits within the mental model is accepted, anything that doesn't is dismissed. Often, the business mental model is shared across the entire organization. It becomes the dominant logic and narrative about the business. And in environments with low levels of heterogeneity across firms, the business mental model also becomes shared across the industry. As a result, you become trapped within your mental model.

It takes an outsider to break through these conventions. As one easyJet executive commented on the company's unusual way of doing business in the airline industry: 'We didn't know it was impossible, so we did it.'

Hire for diversity

Diversity is your best defence against myopia. The way to break through a set mental model is to bring in different ones. Do you find yourself in an environment where all your colleagues have worked in the same industry (or even the same company) for years? It's no surprise then that a common mental model has emerged, and that it is difficult to change. By hiring a diverse set of people, you can make sure new, deviant voices are brought in. This can be done by hiring from outside the industry, by encouraging diversity in demographic profile or, even better, hiring from the same profile as your customers. In a B2B environment, this means hiring people who have experience in your customer's industry instead of your own. Like a Trojan horse, they will make sure that the customer perspective comes forward.

Resource imprisonment

There are two types of innovations: the ones that build on existing competences and those that destroy them. Competence-enhancing innovation builds upon and reinforces existing competences, skills and know-how; competence-destroying innovation makes them obsolete and overturns them.[9] It is easier for organizations to acquire totally new competences than to adapt an existing one to competence-destroying change. It is easier to start from scratch than to shift gears within an existing organization. This is because of the 'stickiness' of competences, implying that companies are to a large extent 'stuck' with what they have. The flip side of having strong competences is that companies can become trapped: core competences become core rigidities.[10] This is the 'competence trap'.

Business model innovation fits within a type of innovation that is 'competence-destroying'. This creates two difficulties. First, the fact that existing competences become obsolete is usually threatening to the balance of power within an organization. People who have built careers linked to these competences see their value greatly diminished and will resist vehemently any move in that direction. The turf battles that result paralyse an organization. For example, how could any trained engineer, with 20 years of experience in chemical technology, be happy about making the switch towards digital technology? Second, the longer a company is active in an industry, the more it has established firm routines that make it harder to explore new opportunities.

The tyranny of current markets

It is often very difficult to turn around an established pattern of resource investment. Firms allocate resources for initiatives that benefit the stakeholders which provide the resources the firms need in the short run to survive. The demands of a firm's current customers, as one of the main stakeholders, thus shape the direction in which innovation development unfolds. As business model innovation often targets new market segments, it loses out.

Enemy number 2: Self-sabotage

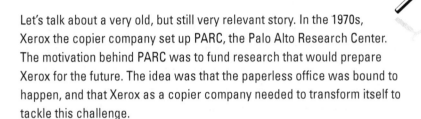

Let's talk about a very old, but still very relevant story. In the 1970s, Xerox the copier company set up PARC, the Palo Alto Research Center. The motivation behind PARC was to fund research that would prepare Xerox for the future. The idea was that the paperless office was bound to happen, and that Xerox as a copier company needed to transform itself to tackle this challenge.

Some of the world's most brilliant scientists were brought together and given unlimited freedom to explore the office of the future. They were tremendously successful. PARC was the creator of the personal computer, the mouse, the graphical user interface and an early version of a computer network, using e-mail to communicate. The researchers at PARC were way ahead of their time, and Xerox sat on a treasure of inventions that we now know changed the world. In spite of that, none of these inventions ever became known with a Xerox label on them. None were commercialized by Xerox itself.

When IBM completely changed its approach to innovation at the beginning of the 2000s it was driven by the finding that in recent years it had developed 29 new technologies, but had not extracted any value from them because it failed to commercialize as aggressively as newcomers did.

The recent demise of Kodak is a cautionary tale against holding on too long to your old business. The failure of Kodak however had nothing to do with being late to the game – it had everything to do with not committing to the game. Kodak had developed a digital camera early on, and was very well aware of the emergence of digital technology. However, there never was full scale commitment to bet on the new technology to the detriment of the old. Too many vested interests made it impossible for Kodak to make the switch.

Blockbuster failed against Netflix because it was hesitant to switch to a subscription model that would make the highly profitable late fees obsolete. It took seven years for Blockbuster to mount any significant response to Netflix.

The examples of Xerox, IBM, Kodak and Blockbuster have something in common. They highlight the fact that the failure of incumbents is not being too late – it is doing too little. It's often a misunderstanding to assume that the incumbent failed to invest. When we look more closely, we see that the incumbent did in fact participate, but not wholeheartedly.

New business is often more uncertain in terms of financial returns than the established business. And sometimes it is definitely less profitable from a relative profit viewpoint. This was the case when Kodak was looking at making the transition to digital photography. As one Kodak manager commented: 'Wise businesspeople concluded that it was best not to hurry to switch from making 70 cents on the dollar on film to maybe 5 cents at most in digital.' Companies can often earn more attractive profit margins by extending their presence in the established business than venturing into new territory. This creates 'asymmetries of motivation': whereas a new entrant may be motivated to push forward (any margin is better than no margin at all), incumbents usually find it more interesting to invest further in the established business. Moreover, the existing business probably requires a lot of resources to remain afloat against competition. There is a permanent pull for resources from the core business. And when push comes to shove, the core business often wins in the battle for resources.

Xerox did everything according to the book. It created room for innovation, allocated people to it and freed them up from any other concern. But it made one critical mistake: when it came to commercializing what it had developed, it hesitated. Why threaten an existing business? Rather than jumping in, it dipped its toe in the water. Ginni Rometty, head of IBM's consulting business remarked: 'New businesses that are a threat to the existing business model are either dumbed down or starved by the larger business.'[11]

As a result, companies self-sabotage their innovation initiatives by not wanting to commit the resources that are necessary to compete. This happens even more when the driving force for the innovation is only to support and leverage the core. For example, if you add services only to promote product sales and it does not work, the new business is starved to death even though it has potential on its own. We call this 'the tyranny of the core business'. The result is self-sabotage of innovation initiatives. To protect against the tendency to self-sabotage, resources for innovation initiatives need to be ring-fenced and protected, and the arguments against cannibalization should never be used to limit investments in new initiatives.

About hungry puppy dogs and fat cats

Myopia, sticky mental models, fear of cannibalization, resource imprisonment, self-sabotage, the tyranny of current markets, asymmetries of motivation – the list of barriers to successful innovation from incumbents is long. This leads to what we call the 'fat cat syndrome'. While incumbents often have more money, experience and assets than newcomers, they nevertheless face an uphill battle if they want to deviate from the established business to innovate.

The situation is entirely different for industry newcomers. They have nothing to lose, no vested interests to defend. They have no entrenched mental models. They have no existing business to worry about cannibalizing. They have no existing customers with expectations and competitors to keep up with. They have no existing routine and rigidities to battle. In other words, the legacy that impedes incumbents is absent for newcomers. They are the eager puppy dogs.[12] Smart newcomers take advantage of this. They do not attack head-on but attack in the areas of least resistance by exploiting the sources of inertia of incumbents. As a result, they get time to develop the business and grow stronger. By the time incumbents respond, they face a strong established competitor instead of a vulnerable newcomer.

CASE STUDY

Take the example of Salesforce.com. When Marc Benioff launched the CRM provider in 1999 he did not focus on the big corporate customers that all existing competitors were hunting for. The initial premise was to make CRM applications accessible to small and medium-sized companies.

He offered a business model based on cloud computing, a new technology of which many still doubted the long-term viability. And the revenue model of Salesforce.com was not based on selling expensive licences but on offering low-entry subscriptions in a software-as-a-service model.

Salesforce.com thus exploited all the traps that hold back existing competitors. It went after a new market segment that was deemed unattractive by incumbents who focused on big corporate accounts. For example, Siebel focused exclusively on customers with more than $1 billion in revenues. Salesforce.com used a subscription pricing model that could potentially cannibalize an incumbent's business if it were to offer it as well. Siebel offered licence fees that ranged between $1,000 and $2,000 per user, while Salesforce.com customers could get started for only $200 a year. Finally, Salesforce.com was a complete newcomer to the industry, not seen as significant by any of the industry analysts and certainly off the radar screen of any of the big incumbents. Whereas these incumbents competed on big customized customer solutions, Salesforce.com offered an easy-to-use standard package with minimal start-up costs. The Salesforce.com offering was hence seen as inferior by competitors.

By all accounts this is a classic story of a hungry puppy dog and a complacent fat cat. Every single one of the reasons that hold incumbents back are present here. And in the end, it was Salesforce.com that benefited from this the most. Its main competitor and market leader Siebel started its cloud initiative in 1999, the same year Salesforce.com was founded. However, the Siebel.com venture was soon seen as distracting too much from the core business and was shut down. By the time Siebel started getting serious about a cloud-based CRM, Salesforce.com had an established footing in the market, attracting bigger and bigger customers. Siebel had to play catch-up. Eventually, this led to Siebel's demise.

How to organize to enable new business creation

Initiatives to launch new business models from an established organization often fail before they get started. How can you prevent these new business models being suffocated by the existing organization? Conventional wisdom says that it's better to separate the new venture from the core business, to create a separate organizational unit for it, with the freedom to operate and allowing for different processes, structures, and cultures. The reasons for this are all about protecting the new venture from the tyranny of the established business. By behaving like a start-up, the separate venture avoids the asymmetries of motivation that we just discussed. It involves the creation of an independent organizational unit given a mandate and resources to invest in new business opportunities.

Internal venturing entails the investment in technologies and business ideas that originate from within the firm's boundaries. External venturing refers to the investment in external start-ups. Companies make a minority investment and take board seats in the start-ups, similar to what KLM did with Fast Track Company (see Chapter 6). In doing so, there are some conditions for the separation to work, discussed next.

Do not 'wait and see'!

Incumbents often think they can wait and see before they jump on new emerging market opportunities. Only when the market starts to take off and the risk is lower do they enter the market. They bet that they can win the market anyway by leveraging their strengths at the right moment, without having to take the pioneering risk. Indeed, it is not always the first company on the market that eventually wins enduring market leadership (anyone remember Yahoo was once the number one search engine?). Business history is littered with examples of first-movers who were not able to defend their market leadership once bigger players jumped in.[13] Stories like this give incumbents the illusion that they have time on their side, which is indeed the case when they remain close to their core business. In situations where a new market opportunity requires a different business model however, incumbents are outside their comfort zone. The need to acquire or learn new competences and skills makes it harder for incumbents to catch up with first-movers quickly enough. And this is when it is dangerous to assume you can catch up in due course. This is what the story of the demise of Blockbuster clearly illustrates.

More often than not the result is 'too little too late'. The idea that you have the luxury of waiting is nothing but an illusion. The competence trap is to blame: incumbents are at a disadvantage to new entrants when it comes to competence-destroying innovation. Rather than having the luxury of waiting, existing players should work extra hard and extra early to make the shift.

Freedom to operate

When separating innovative ventures, the core organization needs to resist the urge to meddle, or to present the 'meddling' as 'help' or 'sharing best practices'. When a new opportunity requires an entirely different approach, well-meaning executives often try to apply old recipes, even when they are not applicable. New ventures should have the freedom to divorce from the organization, and create a new recipe for success. This is how Nestlé became successful with Nespresso. Nespresso was split off as a separate entity that had total freedom to decide on its own production, distribution, commercial and HR policy, which enabled Nespresso to develop an entirely new business model in the coffee market.

Identify assumptions

Behind every business plan there is a whole set of assumptions. The more you find yourself in unknown territory, the more assumptions and the fewer certainties there are. Established practice is to bury the assumptions and uncertainties deep in the business plan and create an 'illusion of accuracy'. After all, that is what most executives have been trained to do: provide quantitative evidence for a business case and demonstrate the value of a new initiative. A big problem is that companies tend to treat nascent opportunities the same way as they approach established businesses. They want data, even though data on non-existent markets is inherently fictional. The truth is, a lot of important things cannot be measured and a lot of measured things are not important. This is especially the case for novel emerging opportunities that take you further away from the established core business. Revenues from products that stay close to what the company is currently selling can often be credibly quantified – there is an established basis of data and codified knowledge. But proposals to create growth by exploiting entirely new products or business models can't be bolstered by hard numbers.

What we need to do is identify the hidden assumptions and make them explicit. When we are exploring new emerging market opportunities, having a business plan with a lot of assumptions is not a problem. It's an opportunity to set up a plan to systematically convert these assumptions into knowledge.[14] To make knowns from the unknowns, we need to set up smart experiments. The evaluation of a new venture should not be based on its performance, but on its level of learning.

Smart experimenting

For a new venture exploring an emerging opportunity to be successful, it needs to have the flexibility to adapt the business model along the way. Successful new businesses typically revise their business models at least four times on the road to profitability. That means the focus should be on learning to make educated adaptations. In effect, companies have to focus on learning and adjusting as much as on executing.[15]

The learning process is inspired by what we call 'deliberate mistakes': purposeful tests, set up with the goal of testing an assumption. Companies can achieve success more quickly by deliberately making errors than by only looking for data that support the assumptions. The more real-life these tests are, the more accurate the learning. The richest information comes from field experiments. For example, if you want to learn about customers' interest in a potential new product, you could announce it on your website with a 'Keep me informed' banner. The number of people who click and leave their contact information tells you something about the potential demand.

Smart experimenting speeds up the learning process that would unfold naturally as you develop the business. Smart experimenting also optimizes the ratio between the cost of learning and the value of the learning gained. The point is to make small investments that generate high-value learning that allows you to reduce uncertainty and verify assumptions.

As a project progresses, more and more data become available; more information replaces the unknowns. Reliable forecasts are the best indicator that a new business is learning.[16] At that point, assumption-driven planning can make way for conventional business planning.

Fake it till you make it

A working prototype is not necessary to start carrying out smart real-life experiments. Find ways to work around the problem of not having the actual product, and still do realistic market tests. Why not gauge customer interest by putting a 'keep me informed' button on your website? Or create a fake prototype: a real-life user interface with a fake back-end. It looks like it works, but the back-end functionality is missing. The fake prototype can already be put in users' hands to gain feedback.

Postpone judgement

The process we describe to develop new business models within existing organizations is not one where there is an early decision point on whether to further commit or not. The stories of Nespresso and Onstar clearly illustrate how success is often a long time in the making. They also demonstrate that conventional evaluation techniques would have killed the new ventures early in their existence. When the environment is uncertain, and it's still uncertain what business model offers the right approach to a changing environment, it is extremely difficult to predict success. It is also difficult to judge results early on. We therefore need to postpone judgement.

Match investment with the level of uncertainty

The real potential of the venture is discovered as it develops over time. At every decision point, the information gained should determine the next step. At every point, the level of investment made should match the level of uncertainty that still remains. High uncertainty demands

FIGURE 8.1   Single bet versus strategic experiments

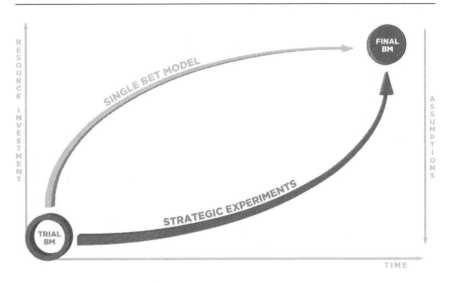

small-scale investments, geared primarily at learning; no irreversible commitments to a particular business model are made. The idea is to preserve flexibility to shift gears when needed. As uncertainty goes down over time, the level of investment goes up; see Figure 8.1.

Enable smart borrowing

Conventional wisdom dictates separating innovative ventures from the core organization so as to give the freedom to explore new business models and deviate from established practices. While this may be true, there is also a clear downside to it. When innovative ventures are kept outside, they cannot benefit from any of the advantages and strengths of the established organizations. In fact, irrespective of access to funding, this means the venture is no different from any other start-up that does not have the backing of a larger organization. This creates a missed opportunity to leverage assets and resources from the core organization that could create a critical competitive advantage for the fledgling venture. Separation therefore has to be combined with mechanisms that link the new venture and the parent firm. By exchanging shared resources, the parent company and the new venture live together and share their strengths.[17] These exchange mechanisms should enable the venture to benefit from the assets of the parent firm, without being restricted by them.

So, there is a level of operational integration required to give new ventures the maximum opportunities to succeed, by using any parent-firm resources that fit their business model. However, the operational integration should not be dictated by the parent company nor should it be inspired by the desire to create operational synergies that lead to lower costs. The only valid reason for creating operational linkages is to enable the new venture to borrow valuable assets that are critical to its business model and that otherwise would be difficult to obtain.

When in doubt: separate!

Organizing for new initiatives means managing a delicate balance between separation and integration. While the urge to create operational synergies may be great, it is better to err on the side of caution and to separate unless it's absolutely necessary to borrow a critical asset from the parent organization. Early on, it is often not clear what business model is appropriate and the details of the ingredients of the business model have not been identified. In that situation, it is advisable to resist the urge to re-use too much of the existing company's business model. Better yet, keep the new initiative completely outside until you develop a more sophisticated understanding of its business model. Only then can you be smart about integrating where possible and separating where needed.

On persistence and patience

One of the hardest decisions a business can face is whether to pull the plug on a new venture. When you know failure is on the horizon, it's better to cut your losses. Nobody will argue with that. However, the difficulty lies in assessing whether failure is in fact imminent. Apple famously cut the Apple Newton project, but later it became clear there was a large market for a personal digital assistant.

In a rapidly changing environment, in which it is unclear what business model or technology is needed to thrive, it is almost impossible to assess failure or success. Failure is often part of the road to success. While a well-considered smart experimentation process can often shorten this cycle, innovators still need to tolerate failure and struggle. However, persistence in finding the right formula for success is entirely different from stubbornness in sticking to the original plan. Decision makers often fail to adjust their initial expectations, even when new information makes it clear that the original plan will not work. This leads to 'escalation bias': an ever increasing commitment to the wrong course of action, which blocks the trial-and-error process that we need. What we need is persistence in adapting the business model, and patience until the right formula for success is found.

To prevent escalation behaviour, we can adopt the following strategies:[18]

- Change the organizational structure so that continue/stop decisions are made by someone with no prior involvement in the project and no conflict of interest.
- Use *a priori* defined stopping rules that are based on objective data.
- Change the incentive system so people are rewarded for changing plans, not for sticking to them regardless.

In short

- The viewpoint and learning we obtain from using the wide lens need to be converted in new business models. These new business models enable companies to adapt to new realities and design the right business model for a changing world. For that, we need to leave behind the legacy of what made us successful in the past and be willing to invest in the future.
- Successful business model innovation is driven from the market.

- The fear of cannibalization should not drive investment decisions. Instead of fearing cannibalization, fear obsolescence.

- A regular business plan process is useless when we try to invent the future. The number of unknowns is too big to be able to formulate a business plan with any sense of confidence in the numbers. We need to highlight the unknowns and assumptions, and set up a process to tackle them.

- Don't assume that a new formula for success will be apparent right away; it's more likely to be a process of trial and error. A smart experimenting strategy enables fast learning and speeds up the trial and error process. We need persistence in adapting the business model, and patience until the right formula for success is found.

- Smart borrowing allows new ventures to coast on the strengths of the established business, without being suffocated by them.

Get started

- Set up separate ventures to enable new business models.
- Don't let the objectives and priorities of the core organization drive the resources that these new ventures receive.
- Adapt the decision-making process to deal with the inherent uncertainty in the wide lens.
- Develop a rigorous hypothesis identification process.
- Invest in strategic experiments to test these hypotheses.
- Where a new venture can benefit from the assets of the core organization, enable operational linkages.

Notes

1 Vardello, H (2013) How the milk industry went sour, and what every business can learn from it, Forbes.com, January

2 http://www.businessinsider.com/the-success-story-of-chobani-yogurt-2013-5#ixzz2Vh0pYKoZ

3 Osterwalder, A (2010) *Business Model Generation*, Wiley, New York

4 Johnsen, M *et al* (2008) Rethinking your business model, *Harvard Business Review*, December

5 Chandy, R K and Tellis, G J (1998) Organizing for radical product innovation: The overlooked role of willingness to cannibalize, *Journal of Marketing Research*, 35, November, 474–87

6 Netflix, *Harvard Business School Case*, 9-607-138

7 Aaron, S (2004) Movie mania, *Strategy & Innovation*, January-February

8 Hastings, R, Netflix blog, September 2011

9 Gatignon, H *et al* (2002) A structural approach to assessing innovation: Construct development of innovation locus, type and characteristics, *Management Science*, 48, 9, 1103–22

10 Leonard-Barton, D (1992) Core capabilities and core rigidities: A paradox in managing new product development', *Strategic Management Journal*, 13, summer, 111–26

11 O'Reilly, C A (2009) Organizational ambidexterity: IBM and emerging business opportunities, *California Management Review*, 51, 4, 75–99

12 The labels 'puppy dog' and 'fat cat' originate from a 1984 article in *The American Economic Review* by D Fudenberg and J Tirole, 'The fat-cat effect: the puppy-dog ploy and the lean and hungry look'.

13 Markides, C and Geroski, P (2004) *Fast Second: How smart companies bypass radical innovation to enter and dominate new markets*, Jossey-Bass, San Francisco, CA

14 Rita Gunter McGrath calls this 'discovery driven planning'; see McGrath, R (1995) Discovery driven planning, *Harvard Business Review*, July-August. Discovery driven planning bears a lot of resemblance to the approach advocated by V Govindarajan and C Trimble in, 'Strategic innovation and the science of learning, *MIT Sloan Management Review*, winter 2004. A very similar idea was popularized by Al Ries' book, *The Lean Startup: How today's entrepreneurs use continuous innovation to create radically successful businesses*, published in September 2011 by Crown Business Publishing, as well as Steve Blank's *The Startup Owner's Manual: The Step-by-step guide for building a great company*, published by K & S Ranch, Kansas, in 2012.

15 Johnsen, M *et al* (2008) Rethinking your business model, *Harvard Business Review*, December

16 Govindarajan, V and Trimble, C (2005) Building breakthrough businesses within established organizations, *Harvard Business Review,* May

17 Gilbert, C *et al* (2012) Two routes to resilience, *Harvard Business Review,* December

18 Biyalogorsky, E *et al* (2006) Stuck in the past, why managers persist with new product failures, *Journal of Marketing,* 70, 108–21

Collaborate in flexible ecosystems

"The best way to predict the future is to participate in it.

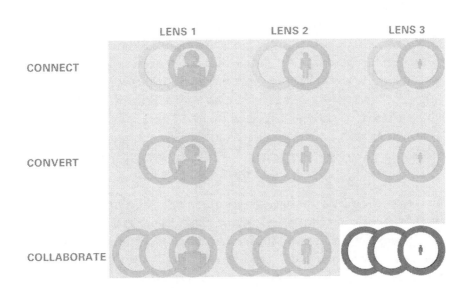

CASE STUDY

Janssen is the global pharmaceutical component of Johnson & Johnson (J&J), a world-leading life sciences and consumer healthcare company. Since its foundation in 1953 by Dr Paul Janssen, a prominent Belgian pharmacologist and medical doctor, Janssen Pharmaceutica has discovered and marketed many breakthrough prescription medicines in areas like diabetes, HIV/AIDS and rheumatoid arthritis. Like all other major players in the pharmaceutical industry, at the start of the new millennium Janssen was confronted with a number of potentially game-changing challenges, leading to an ever more competitive healthcare environment.

The previous blockbuster drug business model is under pressure. The old approach focused the majority of a company's investment on creating blockbuster product franchises – an approach that has been tremendously successful for the big pharma players, in an industry with above-average profitability rates. But that profitability is going down, due to multiple factors: declining R&D output, rising costs of commercialization, shorter exclusivity periods and increasing payer/buyer influence. It is becoming more and more difficult for pharma marketers to gain access to physicians, who are themselves increasingly influenced by payers and legislators, and by patients taking an active role in their prescription decisions. Healthcare policy makers and payers are increasingly mandating or influencing what doctors can prescribe. Patients become ever more empowered and active players in their treatment. The number of people using the internet to find healthcare information has increased dramatically and patients arrive at the doctor's office armed with information. All of these signs indicate that a transformation of the healthcare ecosystem is taking place, moving the pharmaceutical industry 'beyond the pill'. It is this last phrase that became Janssen's new strategic mantra.

The avenue for the future was surely not going to be the same as in the past. Janssen realized that instead of being product-focused, it had to become solution-focused: being patient-centric means not just focusing on drugs. Contemporary healthcare solutions incorporate prevention, diagnostics and patient services, treating patients as partners in a healing process, so that they can be actively involved, leading to a higher chance that they will stick to their therapy and be successful with it.

With this prospect in mind, Janssen Pharmaceutica conducted a scenario planning exercise for its most important markets.[1] The logic of this exercise was: even if it was not possible to forecast the future of healthcare with any degree of certainty, by depicting the potential set of scenarios that could develop, taking into consideration the most driving uncertainties in the healthcare ecosystem, the company would be better prepared for what might come. Based on this exercise, some different opportunity spaces were identified.

In the future, technology would give rise to a new ecosystem of producers and consumers. Participating in this world would require Janssen building an integrated consumer-centric disease management system instead of a drug portfolio and pipeline. It became clear that, to be prepared for the future, Janssen needed to develop a new set of capabilities. To build these capabilities, Janssen concluded that it would be necessary to collaborate with other players that are predominantly active in biotechnology and bioinformatics. With this in mind, Janssen created the Venture & Incubation Centre. This new centre had the task of identifying and supporting projects that focus on new business models, products and services. In addition to these capability-building objectives, the Venture & Incubation Centre served to promote a business development culture and competence throughout the Janssen organization, and to deploy, retain and attract entrepreneurial talent. Projects, called New Business Opportunities, need to pass the following strict criteria to be accepted into the process: a) they must be new revenue-generating products, services, assets or business models, in markets with significant potential; b) they must require high levels of collaboration, either cross-departmental, cross-sector or cross-company (also external to J&J); and c) they must provide a solution in one of the opportunity spaces it had identified for the future.

One of the projects being incubated is Healseeker, a computer game designed to help 8–12-year-old children with ADHD learn particular skills that they find hard developing given their condition; these include time management, social behaviour and planning. The game uses the idea of implicit learning: learning goals are taught with the help of the tasks in the game. The project is being realized with cooperation of Ranj (a software developer), Yulius (a private psychiatric clinic) and Zitstill (a patient association for ADHD). Yulius provides scientific theory, Ranj is programming the game based on the concept from Yulius, and Zitstill will be used as an entry channel into the market.

Healseeker is a perfect illustration of the kind of opportunities Janssen is exploring through the incubation centre. It allows it to develop new offerings to patients that are solution-driven instead of product-driven. Janssen works with other players to make it possible to create these new solutions without having to develop all of the necessary capabilities in-house. It also helps Janssen gain experience with a totally new category of offerings, ie game-based healthcare solutions. The learning it gains from this experience can help it develop similar games for other diseases or patient groups.

Explore new horizons

The story of Janssen shares a lot of familiarities with what many industries are undergoing nowadays. They're thriving in an established industry. All players have converged towards a uniform business model. They focus on battling one another, playing a game that is very familiar to them. But increasingly they feel that the game board itself is changing. At first, they ignore and minimize it, until the effects become tangible. They're not confronted with a sudden sweeping change, but a number of emerging trends that together have a profound influence on their business model. At first they think change is slow, then suddenly the pace is accelerating much faster than expected. All players begin to realize they will have to change, but only people with a crystal ball can predict exactly what to do and when is the right time to do it.

A number of dynamics describe what is happening:

- changes in the market drive changes in the industry;
- the long-term effect is unclear;
- it is uncertain what the right avenue for the future is;
- any future scenario will require new capabilities.

The answer from Janssen contains a few important ingredients. First, the strategy it deployed is driven from understanding the changes in the market, which makes it move beyond the product to thinking more about customer solutions. Second, the strategy is built on a number of plausible scenarios, some close to the status quo, some entailing a major change. Without committing to a single strategy, Janssen prepares itself for a number of possible futures. Third, stronger collaboration with external partners is imperative. It is much faster to work with others that possess the skills you require to make a new opportunity happen than to try to develop them yourself. And fourth, a separate unit is created to prepare the broader organization.

These four ingredients are the cornerstones of the collaboration strategy behind the third lens. Uncertainty is demanding that companies flexibly reconfigure their activities, assets and capabilities so as to explore new opportunity spaces. Customers increasingly demand complex solutions that cannot be delivered by a single firm. Changing the perspective from what a single firm can do to what an entire ecosystem of firms working together can do, makes us realize that this is the avenue of the future.

Within the third lens, we explore a completely new opportunity space that requires us to rethink our existing business model. New competitive realities often call for radically different resources, and it is difficult to predict exactly what the requirements for the future will be. If you fail to understand what resources are needed to compete in the future, you will fail to identify the ecosystem that possesses the required set of resources and capabilities. If you have doubts about what resources you need to achieve to survive and thrive, the first step is to get a better understanding. That understanding often will not come from a formal strategic planning process but from participating and learning.

It is possible to navigate this new environment by setting up ventures and smart experiments, as we discussed in the previous chapter. But to build agility and speed, it's better to work together than to go at it alone. In Chapter 6 we raised the option of whether to build, borrow or buy missing resources and capabilities. By working with others, companies can quickly borrow the necessary capabilities without needing to invest the time or the money to build them themselves. At the same time, this creates an opportunity to learn.

Think in terms of ecosystems

A key task is thus to design the ecosystem that will enable the firm to explore new opportunity spaces. An ecosystem is a business network of loosely connected participants with a high degree of interdependency.[2] It is shaped by collaborative arrangements through which firms combine their individual offerings into a coherent, customer-facing solution. Every firm active within an ecosystem follows its unique core logic, creating and capturing the final customer-facing solution. Every firm thus has its own business model, but the sum of the individual firms delivers more than the individual components. The network of individual firms joins forces to align together for a joint market offering to which they all contribute.

Operating in an ecosystem takes the issue of boundaries (determining which activities to undertake within the firm, which to undertake

FIGURE 9.1   Orchestrate the ecosystem

with partners, and which to take to the open market) to a new level of complexity. The relevant unit of analysis for your strategy becomes the ecosystem in which you operate rather than your company alone. This means that a company's success in shaping its future depends on the extent to which it can shape the ecosystem around it. The key capability to develop is the ability to co-opt complementary capabilities, resources and knowledge from the network of firms around the firm.

Operating from the perspective of an ecosystem instead of a single firm offers many advantages.[3] It removes the time, space and resource constraints that create the boundaries for strategic thinking about a firm's future. Instead of thinking about what the company could do, we now think about what the company could do if it joined forces with others. Instead of being limited by what you could accomplish alone, more options are possible if you can borrow from outside parties what you lack to create value for the end customer. These outside parties can be suppliers, complementary organizations, partners, competitors, and so on.

The advantages of thinking about ecosystems instead of the individual company are:

- *Speed.* Working with others enables the firm to exploit new opportunities much faster than it would going it alone. The resource barrier is removed and replaced by the opportunity to borrow any missing resources and capabilities from players who already possess them. If Janssen had tried to develop a game itself, it would first have had to develop the necessary skills. It's a much faster route to work with a company that's already experienced in the field.

- *Flexibility.* Building new capabilities in-house often requires irreversible investments and commitments. By relying on external parties, the company can keep its options open and be much more flexible to change course later on. The company also keeps the flexibility to work with different parties, not having to commit to a single one.

- *Access to a greater pool of knowledge.* By working with others, an entire world of knowledge and experience opens up for the firm to tap into. Instead of relying on its own knowledge, the company can benefit from all of the knowledge and experience of its partners in the ecosystem.

- *Joint forces.* The ultimate goal of the ecosystem is to deliver value to the customer, whether it is directly or jointly with others. Ultimately, all the costs and profits within the ecosystem have to be covered by the end-customers for the ecosystem's products and services. So it is important that the driver of the ecosystem remains the final customer, not the competition between or within rival ecosystems. This means incentives need to be aligned so that all parties benefit from being able to bring a new solution to the ultimate customer.[4]

- *Shaping power.* Companies working together can have a greater impact on the direction the industry is taking than a single firm could have. Think about the ecosystem Apple created by enabling others to develop applications for its phones.

To be successful with an ecosystem strategy the focal firm needs to act as more than a pure orchestrator. It has to contribute one or more critical assets itself that are necessary to develop customer value, otherwise the company falls prey to the 'IBM-syndrome': when IBM wanted to force a quick entry into the fledgling personal computer market, it enabled Microsoft and Intel to supply the key components. With this, IBM also gave away the power in the ecosystem, and was forever kept hostage by the power appropriated by these two players. We need to deserve our seat at the table by bringing in valuable and necessary assets.

To be irreplaceable in the ecosystem, any company that is part of it needs to ask itself what unique, non-substitutable and value assets it brings. The further we move away from known territory, the harder it may be to bet on existing, old assets doing the job we want. There is more to borrow from others than from ourselves.

Agility versus commitment

Do you know upfront what the right model is? Within the third lens, many different scenarios are still possible. Betting on a single model is highly risky. We need to develop not one single strategy blueprint but a number of possible scenarios based on a number of possible opportunity spaces. The agility to change course is more important than commitment to a single course of action. The more we are uncertain about the direction the future is going to take, the more important it is to be agile. We need to create windows of opportunity to many possible avenues.

This is also where an ecosystem approach has advantages. It allows a company to make small-scale investments, and have them amplified by aggregating the combined commitments of the ecosystem partners. This allows companies to sniff out opportunities without the need to go full scale. A vibrant ecosystem can then enable activities and capabilities to be constantly reconfigured in response to new challenges and new directions. It's a way to move fast and explore multiple opportunities at once.

Working with others is not a way to catch up when you are late to the game. Don't cooperate out of weakness. Combining two weak partners doesn't necessarily make one strong entity.

CASE STUDY

The collaboration between Windows and Nokia is largely seen as a way for both players to catch up in the smartphone market. Newly appointed Nokia CEO Stephen Elop faced a critical decision as the Finnish manufacturer lagged behind competitors in an industry where time-to-market means everything. Many firms failed and disappeared from the radar because they could not launch a compelling smartphone in time and keep up with both demand and fast-moving competition from the East. An alliance with Microsoft was the quick fix that Nokia needed – a strategic move that took Elop less than five months to materialize. In fact Elop said: 'We are moving faster through this partnership than we have ever done before'.

This example shows that collaborating with others instead of working on your own can be a way to speed up implementation. But not finding a suitable partner should not be used as an excuse to delay moving into new areas. The reason to collaborate is that it has strategic advantages that enable you to participate in new strategic directions very early on, with small-scale commitments.

In short

- When we explore new opportunity spaces at the edge of our current business, it is hard to predict the future.
- Better than trying to predict the future is to prepare for a number of different scenarios and to explore different potential business models.
- Working with others enables a company to move fast, keep options open and benefit from others' capabilities.
- Instead of thinking about individual companies competing, it is more relevant to think about ecosystems competing.

Get started

- Set out your missing capabilities so as to explore a new opportunity space.
- Set up multiple collaborations with a range of partners to fill in the missing capabilities.
- Don't commit to a single ecosystem.

Notes

1 The story of Janssen can be found in Van Dyck, W and Aelbrecht, T (2010) Going beyond the pill: Business transformation through corporate venturing at Janssen Pharmaceutica, (eds) Silberzahn, P and Van Dyck, W (2010) *The Balancing Act of Innovation*, 233–49, Lannoo Publishers

2 Adner, R (2006) Match your innovation strategy to your innovation ecosystem, *Harvard Business Review,* 84, 4, 98–107

3 Williamson, P J and De Meyer, A (2012) Ecosystem advantage: How to successfully harness the power of partners, *California Management Review,* 55, 1, 24–46

4 Adner, R (2013) *The Wide Lens,* Portfolio Trade, New York

The playbook for enduring customer-based growth

Three essential capabilities

Companies rarely die from moving too quickly and they frequently die from moving too slowly. **REED HASTINGS, CEO NETFLIX**

Driving customer innovation fundamentally entails innovating the entire company around the customer. The first capability for customer innovation is to connect with the market and to constantly bring the outside in. There are three steps in developing the capability to connect with the market. In each of these three steps we deploy three different lenses.

Lens 1 is focused on existing customers. By tightening the bonds with their customer base, companies make sure there is a continuous feedback that allows them to stay tuned to changing customer demands and generate the most relationship value out of their customers. They do this through five different practices:

1 a constant feedback loop;

2 immersive customer understanding;

3 using every source of information they have;

4 using customers as sources of ideas; and

5 using customers as developers.

Lens 2 zooms out from the current product range to the entire customer journey. Instead of trying to understand needs related to their own products, customer innovation is in the entire path customers are taking to accomplish a certain outcome that the product helps them to realize. Every step of that path is an opportunity to add value for customers, and to innovate.

Using *Lens 3,* the company zooms out even more to capture the signals from emerging change on the periphery of the market. Using the third lens allows companies to escape the customer competitor traps.

Constantly zooming in and out using the three lenses, firms develop a comprehensive market orientation that enables them to build deep customer connections now, and at the same time anticipate new market evolutions. The three lenses we use range from being reactive to being proactive. The first is about reacting immediately to imminent shifts in customer requirements. It's about keeping a constant eye on the needs of existing customers and bringing those customers closer to the organization. The second lens allows us to see a broader perspective from the customer's point of view: it's not about our products or services, it's about what customers try to accomplish through our products and services. With the third lens we are anticipating the bigger changes that are going to affect our market in the future.

Companies constantly need to deploy the three lenses to stay abreast of customer needs and market development. The heightened awareness and customer vigilance creates a wealth of knowledge sources to tap into. But they serve no purpose if the company is not using the knowledge they create.

Step 1 – Connect, is about waking you up, about developing a constant alertness. Step 2 – Convert, is about converting that alertness into action. There is no point in connecting with customers and detecting new evolutions in the market if you are not willing to change your offering as a result. This happens at three levels that correspond to the three lenses discussed in every part of this book. Each of these levels has a deeper impact on the company's business model and stretches the organization further away from its existing state.

Lens 1 is about constant micro-innovation. 'A day without change is a day wasted' is the mantra. This change is about constant improvement to respond to customers better. Here, we focus on serving existing customers better, using our existing business model.

Lens 2 is about keeping the focus on customer solutions. Innovations are driven by solving customers' problems, not so much by exploiting one's own capabilities. To do so, companies need to stretch further than their comfort zone.

Lens 3 is about renewing your business model to reach new markets or market segments. Customer innovation means that organizations embrace this type of innovation wholeheartedly, without the fear of cannibalization. To avoid organizational backlash, they cleverly deploy different organizational structures, depending on how deep the change goes into the existing activity system of the company.

Step 3 is about collaborating to enable innovation. Within Lens 1 we go deeper again inside the company, and enable the firm to create a culture of deep customer connections. Success resides in successfully mobilizing two partners: the customers and the employees. Using Lens 2, we develop a view that is broader than our own products, and extends towards the customer's goals and the process they use to accomplish them. Creating new customer solutions hence often requires that firms step out of their comfort zone and develop new competences. These competences may be beyond their own limits to develop, or develop fast enough. In that case, it is better to join forces with somebody else who possesses the required resources or competences. Resource gaps are filled in by collaborating with partners. To implement customer innovation, companies thus leverage others' strengths; however, they also leverage their own strengths to make sure they remain in the driver's seat as part of the ecosystem they operate in. The assets they leverage can be technology-based but also market-based. We have discussed several cases where market-based assets, both downstream and upstream, become the source of competitive advantage. These market-based assets can be access-, information- or experience-based. Collaborating is thus about exploiting one's own assets to balance the contributions of others to the entire ecosystem that delivers a customer solution.

What is the value of looking at the overall picture of the connect-convert-collaborate framework? What the framework highlights is how each of these steps are intrinsically linked to one another. Connecting with customers needs to lead to converting, ie to changes and innovations, otherwise it's an empty exercise. Creating innovations in turn forces us to collaborate internally and externally. The three steps – connect-convert-collaborate – represent a chain of events that is as strong as its weakest link. Seeing the steps in connection to one another forces us to assess whether we organize ourselves to make sure that the connections happen. It warns against isolated initiatives, with disappointing results as the inevitable outcome.

Diagnose your organization

The three lenses differ in terms of the extent we can see clearly. They range from a laser-like focus when using Lens 1 to blurry images when using Lens 3. Using the three lenses we trade-off depth and breadth of the image we create. Lens 1 is about building deep connections with existing customers. Lens 2 is about developing a view beyond our own products and services towards the role they play for customers. Lens 3 is about intense curiosity about new emerging opportunities on the periphery of our current market. Table 10.1 highlights the key differences between the lenses.

TABLE 10.1 Key differences between the lenses

	Lens 1	Lens 2	Lens 3
Unit of analysis	Firm	Value chain	Ecosystem
Time horizon	Short term	Mid term	Long term
Type of innovation	Incremental	Solution	Business model
Key collaborator	Customers and employees	Customers and suppliers	Suppliers, competitors and partners
Level of commitment	Defend and improve your current market position	Aggressively hunt for opportunities to add value for customers	Place selected bets with the aim to learn and reduce uncertainty
Uncertainty	Low	Medium	High
Strength to nurture	Culture	Integration skills	Agility
Key capabilities to leverage	Culture and customer connections	Technological and market-based assets	Ecosystem orchestration and learning skills
Competitive advantage	Internally embedded	Integrated and controlled	Jointly built

Key questions to ask about the three lenses are:

- *Do we actively deploy all three?* Every company should make a conscious effort to develop processes that direct attention and resources to each lens. The three lenses do not represent a chronological evolution: we need a parallel effort in all three.

- *Are we state of the art in all three?* Every chapter in this book highlights the key considerations to make in every step of the connect-convert-collaborate chain.

- *Do we have the right balance of resources and attention for all three lenses?* The danger of myopia is always around the corner when focusing too much on the first lens. But betting all on the third lens means we don't put enough resources in incremental innovation.

- *Do we close the cycle?* Exercising the three lenses is a continuous cycle. The third lens expands our view, and by converting it into new customer offerings, we make sure to bring this lens in closer focus. What once was the third lens eventually becomes the first.

Driving the organization towards customer innovation cannot be relegated to a single department or function. It starts at the top but it is not a job for a lone crusader. Fundamentally changing the company depends on the deep commitment of the CEO. Implementing customer innovation is not a one-time thing. It's not a project, it's a deeply rooted strategic imperative that requires constant focus.

No one would call becoming truly customer focused easy, but it is the only way to outpace others, both newcomers who appear out of nowhere to seize the limelight as well as current competitors. Ultimately, the ability to innovate the company around the customer becomes the ultimate core capability. At that point, customer innovation becomes the source of competitive advantage. Employees become programmed to creatively and constantly innovate to keep the enterprise indispensable to customers. Successes can be repeated, and enterprises can continue renewing themselves in their quest for profitable growth in futures they themselves have shaped.[1]

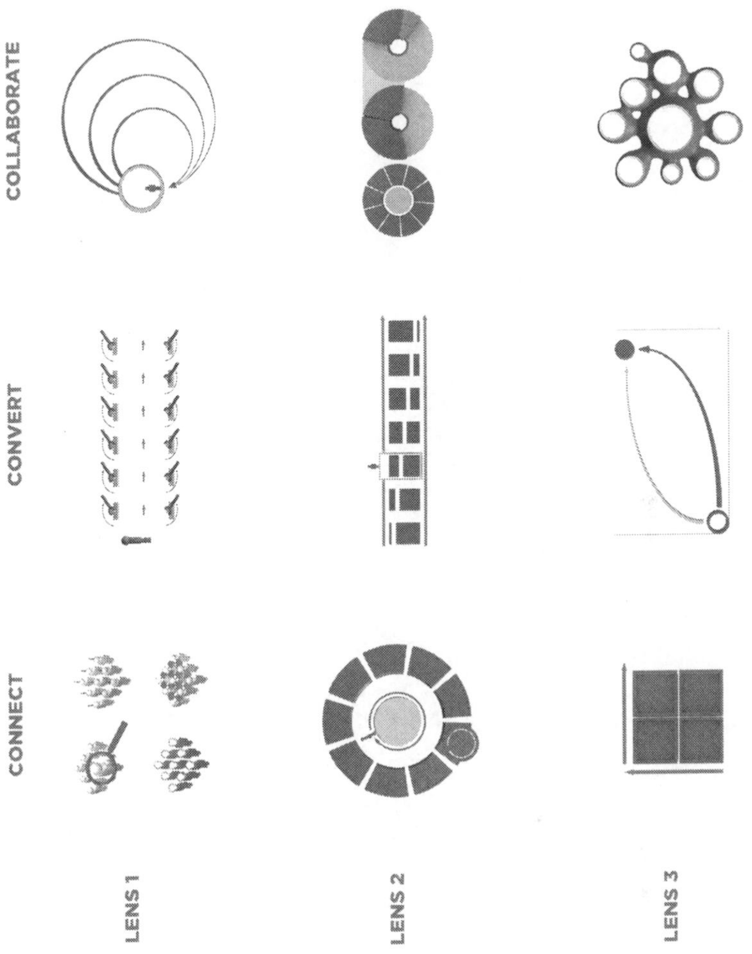

FIGURE 10.1 The playbook

Note

1   Vandermerwe, S (2004) Achieving deep customer focus, *MIT Sloan Management Review,* spring

INDEX

(italics indicate a figure or table in the text)